·BBC TV PRESENTS·
a fiftieth anniversary celebration

TV50

·BBC TV PRESENTS·
a fiftieth anniversary celebration

TV50

Nicholas Moss
foreword by Bill Cotton

BBC Data
Publications

© British Broadcasting Corporation 1986
First published November 1986
Reprinted December 1986

ISBN 0 946358 29 X

Published by BBC Data Publications
4 Cavendish Square, London W1A 1AA

Designed by Annette Peppis

Design Consultant: Haydon Young
Cover Photograph: Chris Capstick

Printed in England by
Netherwood, Dalton & Co. Ltd., Huddersfield

PICTURE CREDITS

All illustrations are from BBC sources, including the Hulton Picture Library, except: p11 Punch; p12 bottom, Neil T. Bestwick Rimington; p16 estate of the late D. R. Campbell; p17 top, Royal Television Society archive; p18 top, T. H. Bridgewater; p19 left, R.C.A., right, E.M.I.; p20 left, Television and Shortwave World; p22 top right, E.M.I.; p24 R. W. Peat and T. A. Coombs; p32 top, K. Critchley; p58 centre, Picture Source; p82 bottom, P. H. Jones; p90 bottom, NASA; p92 MGM/UA Television; p93 top, Press Association; p104 top left, Lorimar; p105 centre right, Metromedia; p108 spread, Associated Press. Technical illustrations on pages 12, 13 and 18 by Alan Burton.

ACKNOWLEDGEMENTS

I am most grateful to William Carrocher and to Tony Bridgewater for their unstinting support and help.

My thanks also to Cherry Alston, June Averill, Elizabeth Balfour, BBC Written Archives Centre at Caversham, John Blakeborough, Dallas Bower, Bob Bright, Ruth Edge, Peter Elliott, Bernard Greenhead, William Gregory, Piers Hawkins, Rachel Hender, Ken Howe, Barbara Kronig, Alan Lafferty, Alan Lawson, Suzanne Lewis, Gerhard Lubszynski, Cecil Madden, Helen McKay, the late Leslie Mitchell, Inge Mitchell, Nicola Painter, Vera Peppis, Barry Read, Jennifer Redman, David Smith, Tim Voore, Roger Wemyss-Brooks.

Nicholas Moss
BBC Television Centre
1986

Nicholas Moss joined the BBC in 1981 as a local radio producer following five years as editor-in-chief of a group of newspapers based in Harrogate, North Yorkshire. After a spell in BBC regional television he took up his present post on the staff of the Chief Assistant to the Managing Director, BBC Television, in March 1985. On behalf of the BBC he has co-ordinated and has had a curatorial responsibility for historical aspects of 'The Story of British Television' exhibition, of which the Corporation is a major sponsor, at the National Museum of Photography, Film and Television at Bradford. The exhibition is part of the anniversary celebrations.

Nicholas Moss is 36 and lives with his wife, Jane, in Ashwell, Hertfordshire.

CONTENTS

FOREWORD

In 1936 when the BBC opened the first full scale high definition television service in the world, the risks could not have been greater.

From the beginning, all those at Alexandra Palace, programme makers, technicians and administrators, were operating virtually in a vacuum.

They were the pioneers, the trail blazers and as such had no colleagues in other television services to whom they could turn for advice. Nor did they have any touchstone by which they could assess results.

The public was familiar with the concept of television from 'Ally Pally' largely through the press; but comparatively few people had seen a broadcast.

So, in spite of their dedication and enthusiasm, those present on opening day, November 2nd, must have wondered just where this new technological wonder would lead them.

They need not have worried. If ever there were a lasting tribute to those responsible for the new medium it lies in the nature of today's television service.

That same pioneering spirit has persisted as programmes and technology have evolved, as audiences have grown and as new areas of development have opened up within the service.

The BBC is proud to celebrate this milestone in its history. I hope that the pictures in this commemorative book will be an entertaining and an informative reminder of some of the faces which have appeared on our screens during the last half century.

Bill Cotton, Managing Director, BBC Television.

A TELEVISION HISTORY

"....television cannot be regarded as an alternative to sound broadcasting; rather in the course of time, may it become a supplementary adjunct thereto."

– advice to potential viewers in 1936.

Switching on a television set today is almost a reflex action with barely a thought for the technology which transforms a blank screen into one of the most powerful means of communication ever conceived.

But a mere fifty years ago, it was the technology itself, rather than the use to which it could be put, that exercised the minds of politicians, scientists and the BBC.

The challenge lay in the development of the appropriate system for the world's first regular high definition public television service. The nub of the early British television story is the race between two of those technologies.

Each, in a sense, represented a different age. On the one hand there was a mechanical process with its hangover from the last century, where scientific progress was such that, for things to work, there were usually moving parts. On the other was a non-mechanical electronic system which, only a few years before, would have been unworkable.

DISTANT ELECTRIC VISION

Although the television service proper started at Alexandra Palace in North London in 1936, the route to 'Ally Pally' as it became known, had its origins considerably earlier.

Scientists had been occupied by the notion of television – a system for converting light into electricity, which some called 'distant electric vision' or 'seeing by electricity' – since the late 19th century. It was an interest prompted by Victorian inventions such as the telephone, the electric telegraph and equipment which would transmit still images by wire. Although several individuals had fertile minds and devised rudimentary television systems the technology did not exist to make their schemes for harnessing electrical impulses fully workable. For one thing, practical television was impossible without valves to amplify small currents.

It was the pioneering work, stemming from the original vacuum light bulb, which developed the valve as an amplifier.

This cartoon by Du Maurier appeared in Punch in 1879. It portrays the then fanciful notion of transmitting live moving pictures down a telephone line.

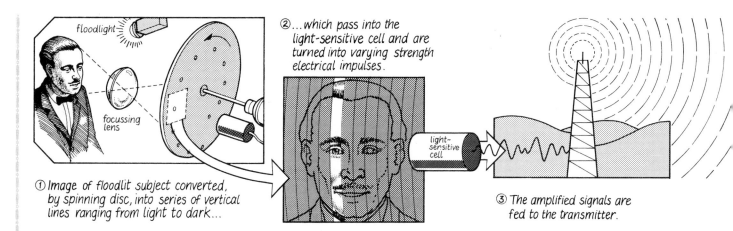

floodlight

focussing lens

① Image of floodlit subject converted, by spinning disc, into series of vertical lines ranging from light to dark...

②...which pass into the light-sensitive cell and are turned into varying strength electrical impulses.

light-sensitive cell

③ The amplified signals are fed to the transmitter.

The first world war and military demands for improved communications involving valve technology led to wireless becoming well established. It was then only a natural step for scientists to try to satisfy a persistent niggle, the transmission of live moving pictures. They were, as always, bound by current progress. So, most pioneers seeking the systems likely to bear fruit, went for a mix of existing mechanical and electrical components. At that stage electronics and other scientific frontiers were yet to be conquered.

There was a well-understood basic principle that the best means of transmitting any image was by devising equipment capable of 'observing' it and breaking it down into smaller parts, a process known as scanning. The parts would then have to be translated rapidly into electric signals, transmitted and then reconstructed in the same position and order at the receiving end, as still happens with television.

The most promising mechanical scanning system was the Nipkow disc, named after its German inventor, Paul Nipkow and patented in 1884. In essence it operated as a rapidly revolving metal disc punched with holes in a spiral pattern around the edge. When looked at it had the effect of appearing to break down a brightly lit object behind it into a series of lines each next to the other, forming a complete image. It could, in theory, be adapted for television by putting a light sensitive device in the path of the image capable of yielding an electric signal varying in strength depending on the light and shade of the original object.

It could not be made to work, however, since the signals were too weak and the amplifying valve had not been invented. In addition, the light sensitive material available, selenium, was inadequate for the task.

The use of sandwich women gained Baird extra publicity for his socks in Glasgow during the 1914-18 war.

THE BAIRD UNDERSOCK for the SOLDIER'S FOOT from Leading Drapers & Hosiers.

THE BAIRD UNDERSOCK for the SOLDIER'S FOOT from all Drapers, Hosiers

THE BAIRD UNDERSOCK for the SOLDIER'S FOOT from all Drapers

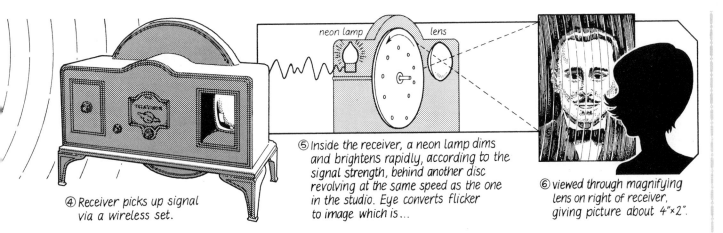

⑤ Inside the receiver, a neon lamp dims and brightens rapidly, according to the signal strength, behind another disc revolving at the same speed as the one in the studio. Eye converts flicker to image which is…

④ Receiver picks up signal via a wireless set.

⑥ viewed through magnifying lens on right of receiver, giving picture about 4"×2".

THE JIG-SAW TAKES SHAPE

It took John Logie Baird, a Scot, to develop the Nipkow process, add to it his own knowledge of valves, optics and mechanics and make it a reality.

Baird, born in 1888 and an electrical engineer by training, had demonstrated his inventiveness from boyhood by rigging up a telephone system to friends' houses and installing electric lighting in his own home. Poor-health over-shadowed his activities and he tried his hand at numerous unlikely ventures including the sale of socks springled with borax to keep the feet warm and jam-making in Trinidad! But television became his primary interest arising from the belief that if one could hear by wireless one must also be able to see by it. By 1923 he was in a position to make a start. Driven by his obsession, Baird devised a television transmission and reception system derived from Nipkow. At the receiving end he organised a neon

lamp to dim and brighten according to the varying current representing the original image and by arranging another disc to spin in front of it, the reassembled picture initially comprising anything between five and 18 lines could be seen through a magnifying lens.

In 1925 he demonstrated his system at Selfridges in London. Results were poor but encouraging and so he formed a company to develop his process. Baird gave the world's first demonstration of true television in London the following year when he televised a person speaking and the head of a ventriloquist's dummy called Stooky Bill. It was a success and he went on to stage a number of

Baird experimenting in April 1925. The object being televised was scanned by the disc in the foreground and the flickering image could be viewed through white disc in the background. The discs in between helped the scanning.

John Logie Baird

George Robey

A scene from 'The Man with a Flower in His Mouth' performed in July 1930. Only one actor's face could be seen at a time because the performing area was so small. The chequer board slid on a rail to allow for changes of actor. The pattern was necessary to avoid upsetting the camera. (l to r) George Inns (fader boy), Lance Sieveking (producer), Gladys Young, Earle Grey, C. Denis Freeman (kneeling), Lionel Millard, Mary Eversley.

promotional events which helped to put television on the map in Britain.

After successive advances including improvements to his photo-cells the image measured about 4 ins. by 2 ins. and consisted of up to 30 vertical lines since this was the number of holes he eventually chose for his experimental transmissions. Various limitations allowed him to produce only 12½ pictures a second thus causing the image to flicker.

His progress led in 1927 to the formation of the Baird Television Development Company, set up to raise capital and to fund further research. Although during the first few years Baird worked with very little help, from 1927 onwards he was able to recruit and rely on an expanding team of competent staff.

In 1928 the firm advertised its three models of receiver, known as the Televisor, for domestic use. They were priced between £20 to £150 but few, if any, were sold. Progress was impossible until regular broadcasts could start. Since the early television pictures, at 30 lines, contained comparatively little signal 'information' the existing medium wave

wireless transmitting equipment was able to cope with them.

The monopoly of public broadcasting was held by the newly-formed BBC and, under its Director General, Sir John Reith, there was great scepticism about the value of Baird's system.

However, after vigorous lobbying the BBC was persuaded, in September 1929, to let the Baird company use its one London medium waveband transmitter for more 30-line experiments, known later as low definition television.

Until the opening of a second transmitter in 1930 there could be no simultaneous broadcasts of sound and vision. So, for a time, items, which were broadcast generally outside the wireless programme hours, could be received partly in sound only and partly picture only.

A range of performances was broadcast from the Baird studio in Long Acre in London including in July 1930 the first publicly televised play in Britain, 'The Man with a Flower in His Mouth', organised by the BBC. For passable picture quality productions were limited largely to head and shoulder camera shots.

Not only did performers have to contend with a new medium but also they had to be heavily made up to compensate for the insensitivity of the equipment and the poor definition. To accentuate their features they wore blue-black lipstick, the same colour on the eyebrows, lashes and sides of the nose and a whitened face. Among the early broadcasters were Gracie Fields (below), George Robey, Arthur Askey and Stanley Holloway.

The singer, Jane Carr wearing the special 30-line make-up for a transmission in November 1932 and (inset) as she appeared to viewers of 30-line receivers.

Many reports were received of programmes being picked up at great distances including Denmark and Italy, not to mention various parts of Britain such as Bradford. A new range of Televisor was now on the market at £26.5s and so great was the enthusiasm for the experiments that people also built their own Televisors from Baird kits costing as little as £7.12s.6d. It is estimated that several thousand were in use.

Baird extended his experiments outside the studio causing great interest by televising the Derby live in 1931. He repeated the operation the following year and also sent pictures of the race for projection on to a screen measuring eight feet by ten feet at the Metropole cinema at Victoria.

Even so, business had not been prospering and by January 1932 the company had been bought out by the Gaumont-British cinema chain. Over the succeeding years Baird was manoeuvred, not altogether unwittingly into a less prominent role in the business.

COMPETITION IN THE WINGS

By the early thirties, the race to perfect television had been speeding up here and abroad. For the Baird Company this had meant, among other improvements, the introduction of yet more sensitive photocells.

Developments had also led to the adoption of a new scanning device. For a short time around 1931/2 the mirror drum, a broad metal band with 30 mirrors around the circumference, was used as an alternative to the Nipkow disc. However, before long it had superseded the disc and coupled with the new photocells it gave more scope for televising larger scenes. It was the system which transmitted the Derby. Mirror drums were also introduced into receivers giving brighter images measuring about 8 ins. by 4 ins.

In 1932, with public interest showing no signs of abating, the BBC became more involved. It installed Baird equipment, initially in the newly-opened Broadcasting House, thus moving programme production away from Long Acre. In August a new series of 30-line experiments started, this time under BBC control and they continued until September 1935.

By 1930 a new range of Televisor was now on the market at £26.5s. This 1931 model had come down to £18.18s. Pictures could be received only if an adapted wireless set was connected to it.

Participants included the record breaking aviators Amy Johnson and Jim Mollison and the singer and dancer Josephine Baker. There were also fashion shows, ballet, boxing, and even, at Christmas 1932, a pantomime, Dick Whittington.

Attention was also being given to improved definition. Baird company research by 1933 had progressed as far as 120 and 180 line pictures derived from a method of transmitting films known as telecine.

Notice the caption drum in the foreground of this view of the control room at 16 Portland Place. The television operation moved here in 1934 because of space shortage at Broadcasting House.

Other British research was making similar mechanical progress.

Meanwhile, German developers, with some of whom Baird was associated, had also achieved 180 line pictures mechanically generated. In the United States they were about to make headway with a 343 line electronic system. Here and abroad much investment was at stake. It was soon to be realised, except apparently by the Baird company, that although mechanical television had been the most practical to date, the future lay in electronics.

ENTER AN EDWARDIAN HI-TECH DREAM

As with the mechanical system, electronics scientists had to devise a method of scanning and so they pursued a proposition put forward in 1908 by a leading electrical engineer, Alan Campbell Swinton (right).

Following the discovery of electrons – 'particles' of electricity – and the invention of the cathode ray tube at the end of the last century, Swinton felt it would be possible to throw an image through a lens onto a light sensitive screen in a cathode ray tube. Then, he argued, if a cathode ray (electron) beam were directed at the image, in the way the eye reads a book, electric signals representing the tones of the orginal subject could be obtained and transmitted in a fraction of a second.

He also proposed that the pattern of signals could be received on another cathode ray tube with a fluorescent screen at one end capable of glowing under an equally rapid electron bombardment related to the original signals. The picture would, he believed, then be recreated as each minute portion of the bombarded screen would glow long enough to deceive the eye into believing that it was seeing a complete, continuous moving picture. His scheme though, was unworkable because, as with Nipkow,

Alan Campbell Swinton

technology had not caught up with him. At about the same time, a Russian, Boris Rosing, had suggested cathode ray reception but from mechanical picture generation. It was more than 20 years before Swinton's idea became a reality partly through the efforts of Vladimir Zworykin, a physicist working in America but born in Russia and a pupil of Rosing.

With the benefit of advances in electronics Zworykin believed that for the high definition picture he

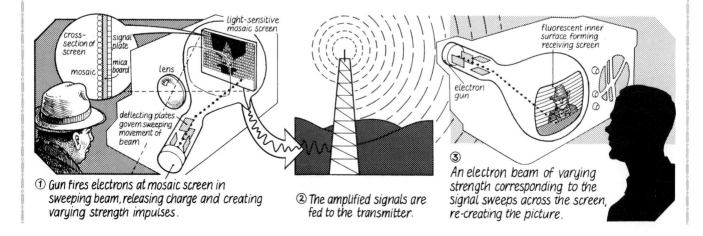

① Gun fires electrons at mosaic screen in sweeping beam, releasing charge and creating varying strength impulses.

② The amplified signals are fed to the transmitter.

③ An electron beam of varying strength corresponding to the signal sweeps across the screen, re-creating the picture.

envisaged, the problem lay in developing a method of generating a sufficiently large electrical impulse on the light-sensitive screen carrying the original image.

His answer was a 'mosaic' screen made up of thousands of microscopic light sensitive-silver globules, each one a separate photo-cell. The result was a camera tube which he called the Iconoscope, reportedly made in 1931.

At the receiving end viewers would watch another cathode ray tube, also designed along Campbell Swinton's lines.

The credit for making cathode ray television a practical proposition is not solely Zworykin's. In Britain in 1931 two record companies, The Gramophone Company (H.M.V.) and the Columbia Graphophone Company joined forces as Electric and Musical Industries (E.M.I.). Through historical connections there was a link between H.M.V. and the Radio Corporation of America (R.C.A.) with whom Zworykin was connected.

The amalgamation meant that not only could the two British firms pool their resources but also that E.M.I. researchers, who were among the top scientists of their day, had access to R.C.A. patent specifications. They were led by Isaac Shoenberg, an inventive, imaginative scientist-entrepreneur. He was also of Russian birth and had been general manager of the Columbia Graphophone Company.

Around 1934, E.M.I. abandoned mechanical scanning in favour of an electronic system, also based on the Campbell Swinton theory, on which they had been working on their own and, originally, unofficially. They categorised the result under the generic name, Iconoscope, later called the Emitron and it was with this independently constructed camera and accompanying transmission system that the firm entered the fray with the Baird operation. The extent to which the E.M.I. and R.C.A. Iconoscopes – very similar devices – were evolved separately remains a matter for conjecture. It seems though that there was little exchange of know-how.

A FIGHT TO THE FINISH

Progress by the Baird company, E.M.I. and others led in 1934 to the setting up of a government committee to investigate developments. Under its chairman, Lord Selsdon, a former Postmaster General, it reported in 1935 that technology had advanced to the point where a high definition public service could start for the London area and recommended the BBC to run it. The estimated £180,000 start-up costs were to be met from the existing 10s. (50p) wireless licence fee.

The committee also recommended that the Baird company and E.M.I. (who had joined with the Marconi company for their transmitter knowledge) should provide the equipment on an equal trial basis. The scene was now set for the final battle between the two technologies.

During 1935 Marconi-E.M.I. were able to offer a 405 line electronic system with fifty pictures a second, virtually eliminating the appearance of flicker.

This was achieved by a process known as interlacing and which forms an integral part of television today. It involved transmitting two sets of twenty five pictures each second. The first set, consisting of the 'odd' lines, 1, 3, 5 etc. was transmitted in 1/50 second followed by the other set, the 'evens' also broadcast in 1/50 second. The two sets together made up the 405 line picture.

The Emitron cameras were mounted on wheels and could even be taken outside with a cable link to the studio. This meant that by the time the service

Vladimir Zworykin   Isaac Shoenberg

opened in 1936 both studio and outdoor scenes could be televised. By linking an Emitron to a projector films, too, could be transmitted.

The Baird company, still committed to mechanical television, had three processes all based on the Nipkow disc, now giving 240 lines definition, the maximum that could be readily achieved and 25 pictures a second 'sequential' scanning i.e. not interlaced. (The mirror drum had now been abandoned as unsuitable for the higher speeds necessary for the improved definition.)

The primary Baird method was the Intermediate Film technique which gave 'almost live' television. Using a camera loaded with 17.5mm. film (half width

An artist's impression of the television installation at Alexandra Palace in October 1936 just before the official opening and (right) the building itself.

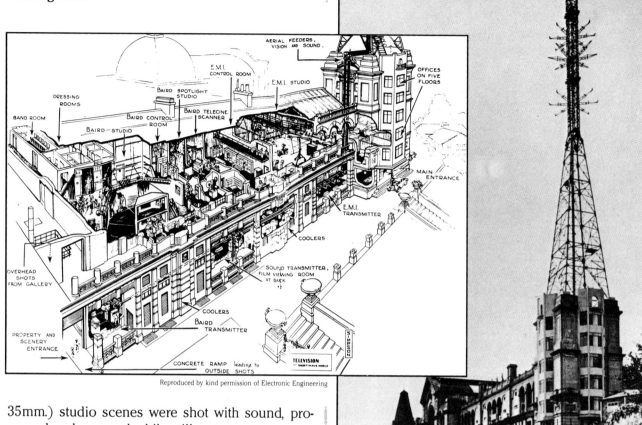

Reproduced by kind permission of Electronic Engineering

35mm.) studio scenes were shot with sound, processed and scanned while still wet.

The whole operation took between 30 seconds and a minute. Apart from not being strictly live it also gave little scope for varying camera positions since the equipment was bolted to the floor. Film magazine capacity limited shooting time to 20 minutes. Wet scanning also led to quality problems, especially with the sound track.

The second and genuinely live part of the Baird system was a small 'spotlight' studio used mainly for announcements. Shots down to the waist only were possible from here. Sitting in a studio in front of a small window the subject was scanned by an intense beam of light flashing through a disc. The reflections were picked up by photo-cells and sent to a transmitter. The whole process was almost identical to that used in the early 30 line experiments, but there was a more subtle version of the special make up.

The third system was the 'telecine' equipment for film transmission.

A Television Advisory Committee was apppointed by the government to make arrangements for the new service. One of its first tasks was to find premises for a television station in which an important factor was the height of the site above sea level. The high definition pictures meant that the medium wave band was now unsuitable for transmissions because it could not carry the necessary sound and vision information. Instead broadcasts would have to be on the larger capacity very high frequency band (V.H.F.); but these were possible only from high ground since the signals would be blocked by land contours if transmitted from too low a location.

Alexandra Palace, a Victorian entertainments centre in North London, 300 feet above sea level, was selected. During 1935/36 a corner of the building, eventually surmounted by a 215 ft. transmitting mast, underwent conversion. It included two main studios, one each for the rival firms as well as all the other facilities necessary for the world's first fully fledged television station.

The first major opportunity for a public demonstration of television arose with the annual Radiolympia exhibition organised by the Radio Manufacturers' Association. Its members hoped to sell the newly developed cathode ray tube receivers but made clear that television was no more than 'an adjunct' not an alternative to sound broadcasting.

The highlight of the demonstration, starting at the end of August 1936 was a variety show called 'Here's Looking at You' with a catchy title song performed by singer, Helen McKay. It is estimated that the promotional programmes, which included newsreels and film excerpts were seen by more than 100,000 visitors. Transmissions, from Alexandra Palace, alternated daily between the Baird and Marconi-E.M.I. systems. Apart from introducing people to the new medium, the demonstrations also started the

Baird's Intermediate Film equipment can be seen in the booth on the left in one of the Alexandra Palace studios. In the background, the Television Orchestra under the talented Hyam Greenbaum, known as 'Bumps'.

cult of the television personality. The BBC had selected three hosts to make the linking announcements. They were Leslie Mitchell (below), an actor, already experienced on radio and about to become a

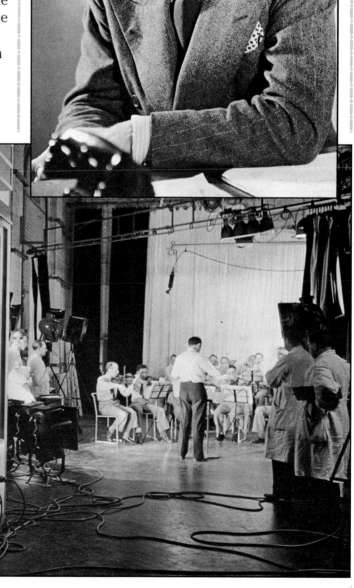

The basic H.M.V. television on sale in 1937. The picture was reflected from the vertical tube into the mirror in the lid.

The television hostesses, Elizabeth Cowell, aged 24 (l) and Jasmine Bligh, 22 in 1936.

Movietone newsreel commentator, Jasmine Bligh and Elizabeth Cowell. They were soon celebrities.

Radiolympia over, test transmissions began in October and, what was to be one of the longest running shows, 'Picture Page', a magazine programme, was first broadcast. A range of guests was introduced to viewers via a mock-up telephone switchboard by a Canadian actress, Joan Miller.

EXIT BAIRD

The official opening of the service was on the afternoon of November 2nd and took place twice; first by the Baird system and then by the Marconi E.M.I. system. It had been planned to use the Baird process only but because of anxiety over its reliability a 'double' inauguration was arranged. There were speeches, a newsreel, a variety performance including a specially composed song called 'Television' sung by Adele Dixon. After the Baird opening viewers were asked to switch their dual-function sets to Marconi-E.M.I. reception.

The audience was small. The prices of sets put them out of reach for most people. Some, giving a

Joan Miller, the 'Picture Page' girl, at the switchboard.

10 ins. by 8 ins. picture, cost up to £100, about the price of a small car. It is estimated that the opening ceremony was seen on no more than about 400 receivers.

But the service was under way and starting, as previously arranged, with the Baird system, the two techniques alternated weekly. There were programmes, mostly live, for two hours a day, from three to four in the afternoon and between nine and ten in the evening daily except Sunday.

Despite good results with Baird telecine which was felt to be better than Marconi-E.M.I.'s film transmission, the Baird company processes as a whole were still unsatisfactory. In an effort to redress the balance Bairds tested an electronic camera, called the Electron, devised by an American, Philo T. Farnsworth, but it was no match for the Emitron and was little used.

Progress in the trial between the two companies was originally due for consideration in April 1937 but with the continuing dissatisfaction with the Baird operation the government, on a recommendation from the Advisory Committee, decided to adopt the Marconi-E.M.I. system sooner. The last Baird transmission was on January 30th.

Baird, despite his remoteness from day to day company activities, was bitterly disappointed at losing the race but continued to concentrate on colour and big screen television for cinemas until his death in 1946. Although he lost the fight it is still his name which many people mistakenly associate with the origin of television in its present form.

The adoption of a single 405 line standard gave the television service considerably more scope for programmes. There was a wide and an ambitious range including variety shows, cartoons, talks, plays, opera, newsreels and fashion parades. But it was the outside broadcast which proved to be one of the biggest draws. The greatest triumph was the televising of the Coronation procession of George VI in May 1937 and estimates of the viewing audience varied between 10,000 and 50,000.

The new King looks towards the camera as he approaches Apsley Gate during the Coronation procession on May 12th 1937.

1

We got to the Alexandra Palace at 9.30 and horribly derelict and dreary it looked, too, - with a tattered poster advertising some dead and gone trade exhibition all across the front.

There was an old man sweeping the leaves and waste paper off the front steps, so I asked if this was the place — ('cos it didn't look it!) "Oh yes sir — this is the place, but the telly-vishun studios is all dahn the other end - they only hoccupies one tower".

Long corridors, enormously lofty, painted walls, and thick silent lino on the floor, fire-appliances at every corner, and lots of blokes in long white coats flitting about and looking horribly like surgeons. Glimpses, through doors marked "Staff Only", of enormous switch-boards and electrical apparatus that seems to shriek "X-Ray".

2

On the studio floor, in addition to a large assortment of scenic furniture, were three or four large pieces of electrical apparatus painted battle-ship grey and mounted on young motor-car chassis. These I correctly assumed to be the cameras but they are boxed in to such an extent that they don't look a bit complicated.

The camera has two lenses jutting out, rather like a very large pair of binoculars, but I fancy that one of them is only a sort of glorified view-finder for the camera-man. At the side of the camera is a little hole into which the camera-man plugs the end of a flex leading to his earphones. By this means the producer can talk to him when at work, without the sound coming into the studio and being picked up by the mike.

3

When I walked into the studio there were about 20 of the white-coated gentry there — some of 'em grooming and petting the cameras, some arranging scenery and lights, but most of them standing in groups talking highly technical jargon. It was agreed that we should try 'Pistol & the French soldier" and "Clementine" to start with, and Jan told me that before the show I was to trickle round to the front and "say a few words". All the cue I should get as to when the camera was coming to life would be this — 👍 from the camera-man.

Well — of all the grim and ghastly jobs — to go and smile sweetly and talk naturally to that black hole of a lens — with the studio as silent as a tomb except for my own voice.

4

I don't mind facing an audience — because I can usually find at least one face that looks interested, and talk to that. And I don't much mind having my photograph taken, even with a cine-camera, because if it's a failure, the negative can be destroyed and the picture taken again.

But this bloody business combines the worst features of both. You try talking to the butt-end of a beer-bottle, and at the same time convince yourself that you are being seen and heard by thousands of people whose only interest for the moment is you.

Television pre-war was a novelty not only to viewers: artistes also found that the experience took some getting used to. Among them was Mr. Wallace Peat who, with his wife, ran the Wessex Glove Puppets. They gave performances in schools of excerpts from the classics and lighter material to whet children's appetites for more serious drama. In November 1937 they were booked for television and, with their puppets, they performed 'Pistol and the French Soldier', an extract from Henry V and a mime to the song 'Clementine'.

Mr. Peat wrote an amusing account to a friend of his day at Alexandra Palace. There is not enough space for the whole letter, only edited sections.

The 'Jan' referred to was the producer, Jan Bussell, a puppeteer in his own right and responsible, with his wife, Ann Hogarth, for post-war successes, such as 'Muffin the Mule'.

Improved outside broadcast cameras covered numerous other events including Wimbledon, the Boat Race and West End shows. In 1938 programme hours were extended during the week and in April Sunday television started. The price of sets fell and some models with a 7 ins. by 5½ ins. screen were now available at under £40. Between the end of 1937 and 1939 sales rose from 2,000 to 20,000, with forecasts of a rapid acceleration. Plans were also being considered to extend broadcasting hours further and to take the service beyond London.

Pre-war television ended as it had begun, during Radiolympia. The service closed abruptly during a 'Mickey Mouse' film transmission on September 1st 1939 on the eve of the outbreak of war. It was felt that the signals from the Alexandra Palace mast would be a natural beacon for enemy aircraft. It was to be seven years before it re-opened.

Full television had lasted barely three years; but during that time the pioneers had laid the ground rules both for programmes and technology which still hold good today.

A studio scene during August 1937 rehearsals for Henry Hall and his dance orchestra.

A typical pre-war studio drama production, 'The Ghost Train', transmitted in December 1937. (l to r) John Counsell, Joan Lawson, Don Gemmell, Alex McCrindle, Clifford Bean, Arthur Young, S.E. Reynolds, Hugh Dempster, Rani Waller, Philip Thornley and Daphne Riggs.

THE TELEVISION AGE DAWNS

In 1943 the government set up a committee under Lord Hankey, a former secretary to the Cabinet, to suggest a policy for post-war television development. On the grounds that the pre-war service had achieved a high standard in the face of what the committee called 'doubt and scepticism' it called for the extension of television to other parts of the country as soon as possible after the re-start of the London service.

It also suggested, among other proposals, improvements to definition, research into colour and the export of television systems abroad. 'Television', it concluded, 'has come to stay'.

The service reopened in June 1946 and brought to an estimated 100,000 viewers the victory parade in

The opening ceremony at the 1948 Olympic Games at Wembley stadium.

The Mall. The restart also coincided with the introduction of a £2 combined radio and television licence.

The Olympic Games in London in 1948 gave opportunity for television again to show its strength at outside broadcasts with many live transmissions from the Olympic centres at Wembley and White City.

The early post war years also saw a rapid broadening of programme horizons, particularly with more ambitious drama such as 'The Gentle People' (1949) in which a replica of a New York waterfront, with water, was built in one of the Alexandra Palace studios.

In 1950 there was the first live outside broadcast from the Continent. 'Calais en Fete' was transmitted in August via a new microwave (high frequency) radio link to Dover and on to London for transmission. Existing under sea cables could not cope with the signal information.

The Dock Green team (l to r) Peter Byrne (Sgt. Andy Crawford); Graham Ashley (P.C. Hughes); Arthur Rigby (Sgt. Flint); David Webster (Cadet Jamie McPherson) Jack Warner (P.C. George Dixon); Geoffrey Adams (P.C. Lauderdale); Moira Mannion (Sgt. Grace Millard).

The first stage of the expansion proposed by Hankey took television to the Midlands in 1949 followed by the North in 1951, where the first programme was called 'Hullo Up There' and Scotland, South Wales and the West in 1952. It brought 81 per cent of the population within transmission range.

Between 1952 and 1955 most of the remainder of Britain was linked to the network so that as well as receiving programmes from London, regions could contribute to national output. About 95 per cent of the population could now receive television and by 1955 the number of licence holders had risen to four and a half million. Three years later the figure had almost doubled and the price of sets had come down in relation to average earnings.

It was, though, the Coronation in 1953 which is regarded as marking the start of the television age. It is estimated that portions of the broadcast were seen by twenty million people in this country watching either on friends' sets or in public buildings. The event was also broadcast in France, Holland and Germany via special connections. Film recordings were sent throughout the world.

The interest shown in continental links, especially for coverage of the Coronation gave rise to one of the most important post-war developments in international television co-operation: the establishment of Eurovision. Set up in 1954, under the umbrella of the European Broadcasting Union, just as continental services were getting under way, television operators in eight countries agreed to exchange programmes. (Thirty one countries are now regularly involved). Perhaps its best-known role in British television is the annual Eurovision Song Contest, first held in 1956 and won by Switzerland.

The rapid post-war expansion soon led to the service's out-growing Alexandra Palace. By 1953 and with approaching 50 hours' broadcasting a week, the BBC had taken over former film studios at Lime Grove at Shepherds Bush in West London, now the base for current affairs programmes.

Andy Pandy pops into his basket after another children's programme.

Throughout the early fifties many popular programmes had their first airing. They included 'Come Dancing' and 'Andy Pandy' (1950); 'What's My Line?' (1951); Billy Bunter (1952); 'Panorama' and 'News and Newsreel' (1954); 'This is Your Life' and 'Dixon of Dock Green' (1955).

For the most part, early programmes were still broadcast live since there was no adequate means of recording them. This proved to be a great drawback since there could be no repeats unless a performance was done a second time. Tests, though, were carried out with telerecordings, made by pointing a 35 mm film camera at a television screen. The Coronation was recorded in this way.

But there were difficulties because the shutters of standard cameras and the scanning action of television were not entirely compatible. To solve the problem, a number of telerecording systems was

devised, none of them ideal. The great advance came with video recording.

One system introduced in 1958, had the video tape running at 200 ins. per second needing a 15,000 ft. reel for just fifteen minutes' playing time. Later the same year an American firm, AMPEX, introduced a different system which increased tape capacity without increasing its consumption. It enabled an hour's programme to be recorded on a 12 ins. spool of 2 ins. wide tape.

The BBC's television monopoly ended in September 1955 with the opening of independent television. The birth of ITV stemmed from the view among a number of Conservative MPs, whose party was in government, that the time had come for competition.

BBC development continued and by the early 1950s plans were also under way for a new television base. Government restrictions on capital spending halted progress for a time but in 1956 work started on the present television centre near Lime Grove at White City, which opened in 1960. Where, 24 years before, Alexandra Palace had offered only two studios each measuring about 2,000 square feet, the new centre eventually had eight studios, with the largest one measuring nearly 11,000 square feet. The turn of the decade also saw the introduction of studios at regional centres throughout Britain.

By 1960 the number of licence holders had risen to ten and a half million. The audience research department estimated that around 40 million people over the age of five had access to a television. Viewers had come to enjoy long running series such as 'Whack-O' (1956), 'Your Life in Their Hands', (1958) and 'Maigret' (1960).

On the engineering front, there were two major advances on the way. Ever since Marconi-E.M.I. had entered the television race with John Logie Baird in 1936, pictures had consisted of 405-lines. They were also in black and white.

The government decided in 1962, following a report, by the Pilkington Committee, that there should be a second BBC channel on higher definition, 625 lines and that it should be colour.

The higher definition had become possible following the development of the shorter wavelength higher frequency equipment necessary to carry the increased picture information. Instead of V.H.F. transmissions they became U.H.F. (Ultra High Frequency).

BBC-2 on 625 lines started, initially in London in April 1964 and gradually spread to the rest of Britain and it offered viewers alternative programmes. The opening night was blacked out by a power failure.

For many years BBC and ITV programmes were broadcast both on 405 and 625-lines. The last 405-line transmitter did not close down until January 1985.

Colour transmissions on 625 lines began on BBC-2 in 1967 followed by BBC-1 (and ITV) in 1969. Colour test transmissions, though, had started more than 10 years earlier at Alexandra Palace in 1955.

Rupert Davies in familiar pose as Simenon's 'Maigret'.

Sir Winston Churchill's coffin at Tower Pier for the journey to Waterloo Station.

Barbara Windsor (Judy), Reg Varney (Reg) and Miriam Karlin (Paddy) get to know a new member of the staff of Fenner Fashions, Bertie the Budgie in 'The Rag Trade'.

The impact of the new service was dramatic. For the first time, audiences saw Wimbledon and Trooping the Colour as they really were. In January 1968 a £5 colour supplement to the standard £5 television licence was introduced and in ten years, colour licence holders rose from 20,000 to 11 million.

The sixties also set new boundaries for television production. In 1965 almost at the close of the black and white era, the State funeral of Sir Winston Churchill was televised with the commentary from Richard Dimbleby. It was regarded as an outstanding outside broadcast and was a massive operation to mount by the standards of the time. Equipment was brought in from all parts of the country and more than

Jimmy Savile introduces the first edition of 'Top of the Pops' in 1964. Inset: John Cleese in his 'Ministry of Silly Walks' sketch in a September 1970 edition of 'Monty Python's Flying Circus'.

thirty cameras were used. The following year saw the televising of England's World Cup victory against Germany. By the turn of the decade audiences had accepted as part of Britain's social fabric programmes such as 'Rag Trade' (1961) 'That Was The Week That Was' and 'Z Cars' (1962) 'Top of the Pops' (1964) 'Till Death Us Do Part' (1966) and 'Monty Python's Flying Circus' (1969). 'Royal Family' and 'The Investiture of the Prince of Wales' (1969) gave millions of people a view of royalty never before thought possible.

Perhaps the most memorable advance of the sixties, in terms of technology and production, was the ability to communicate via outer space. The notion of sending satellites into space as a means of 'bouncing' communications around the globe developed after the last war. But there was nothing powerful enough to thrust a device out of the earth's gravitational pull and put it into orbit. It was not until the launch of the Russian Sputnik 1 in 1957 that serious consideration could be given to the prospects for television links.

Five years later, in July 1962 with the launch by America of Telstar, viewers in Britain saw, for the first time, scenes in the United States transmitted into space and back to earth by microwave link. Improvement led to a number of broadcasts including the 1964 Olympics, recorded parts of which were relayed by satellite from Tokyo to California and then by land line and finally on film by aircraft to Europe. In 1968, with the aid of Eurovision, nearly three quarters of the pictures from the Mexico Olympics were transmitted live in colour via satellite throughout the world.

This was made possible with the BBC's newly developed electronic standards convertor, replacing earlier convertors. The equipment enabled foreign television signals to be converted to different systems instantly.

But it was the moon landing in July 1969 which marked the peak of satellite communication. Black and white pictures from the lunar surface were seen by 14 million people on BBC television alone via two satellites over the Pacific and Indian Oceans. Now, there are numerous satellites regularly bringing pictures into and out of Britain encompassing almost the entire world.

The combined advances in video recording, colour cameras and satellite communication have

1 I WANT TO HOLD YOUR HAND   The Beatles
2 GLAD ALL OVER   The Dave Clark Five
3 SHE LOVES YOU   The Beatles
4 YOU WERE MADE FOR ME   Freddie & The Dreamers
5 I ONLY WANT TO BE WITH YOU   Dusty Springfield
6 24 HOURS FROM TULSA   Gene Pitney
7 DOMINIQUE   The Singing Nun
8 SECRET LOVE   Kathy Kirby
9 SWINGIN' ON A STAR   Big Dee Irwin
10 HIPPY HIPPY SHAKE   Swinging Blue Jeans
11 MARIA ELENA   Los Indios Tabajaras
12 DON'T TALK TO HIM   Cliff Richard
13 I WANNA BE YOUR MAN   The Rolling Stones
14 THE BEATLES (L.P.)   The Beatles
   The Shadows
   (E.P.)   The Beatles
   Elvis Presley
   ALK ALONE   Ger
   Chris Sandf
   (E.P.)   The

Men on the Moon as television viewers saw them.

The Prince and Princess of Wales after their wedding in July 1981.

also helped the development of a system known as Electronic News Gathering (E.N.G.) or Portable Single Camera (P.S.C.).

Traditionally, news or other programme items have been recorded on conventional film, processed at the studios and transmitted through a telecine machine. Or there has been the full-scale outside broadcast. Now, however, with E.N.G/P.S.C. it is possible to shoot on a small colour camera connec-

ted to a portable video recorder. Pictures can either be recorded at the scene on a video cassette or transmitted live with great ease.

Additionally, the establishment of computer technology in television has led to an enormously increased capacity for storing signal information and manipulating it for special effects and other purposes. It has also meant that services such as Ceefax (Oracle on ITV) and programme subtitles are readily available.

If the thirties laid the ground rules for television, then the early post-war period saw their consolidation and the expansion of the service, although Channel 4 did not start until November 1982 following the Annan Committee report of 1977. In turn, the seventies and eighties have witnessed television making the most of the technology which is now available. The pace of advancement is showing no signs of slackening with the BBC very much in the forefront of developments which include higher definition television (around 1250 lines).

There is no sign either in a slackening of public interest in television. For example, while the moon shot was the ultimate outside broadcast in 1969, it was completely eclipsed by the Royal Wedding in 1981. More than 25 million people watched it on BBC alone, 14½ million on ITV and countless more millions saw the event around the world as it happened. That record, too, has been beaten. In July 1985, it is estimated that 30 million people in Britain watched the Live Aid charity concert on BBC Television - more than half the population. About 500 millions more worldwide saw it live via satellite link through the BBC.

The British total can be seen in the context of almost 16 million colour and three million black and white television licences issued, or about 98% of British households with television. On average we spend 25 hours a week watching some of the 400 plus hours transmitted on the four channels.

There can be no doubt that the 60 year evolution of television, from a dim, flickering picture produced through a spinning disc, seen by a handful of people, to today's high-definition, full colour, global network, is a remarkable achievement.

One can only conjecture whether the author of the advice to potential viewers at the 1936 Radiolympia that 'television cannot be regarded as an alternative to sound broadcasting; rather, in the course of time, may it become a supplementary adjunct thereto' ever considered how wrong he might be.

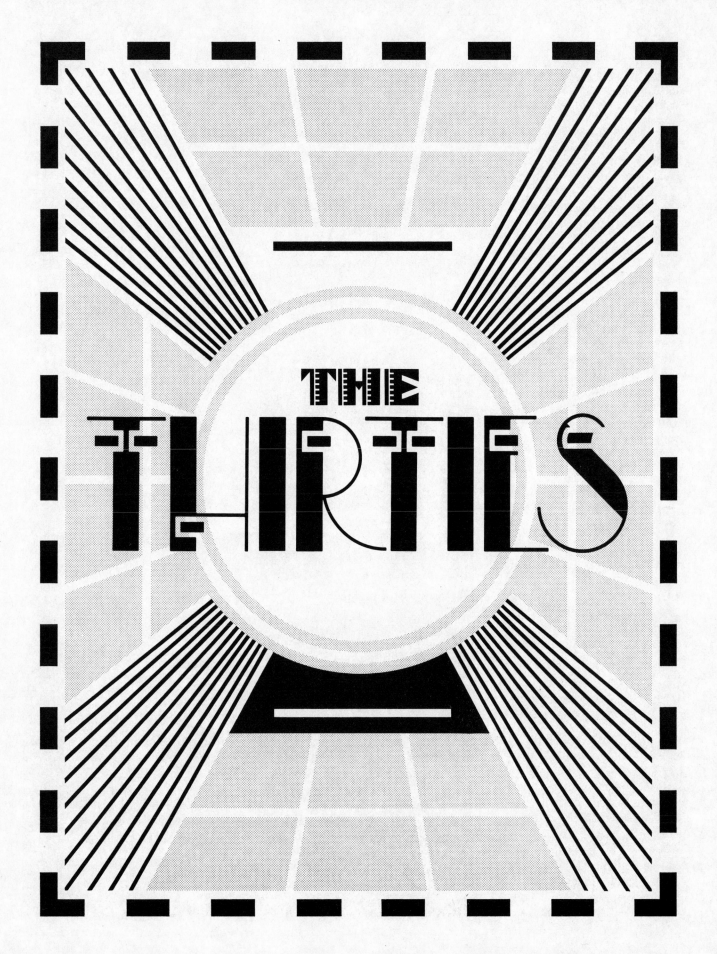

TOP: Jasmine Bligh, one of the three main pre-war announcers, posed before an Emitron camera at Alexandra Palace in August 1937.

BOTTOM: With only about 5,000 sets sold, television viewing was still a minority activity in 1938, especially since reception was restricted to the London area. This set cost around £60, which was expensive for the time. The picture was reflected through a mirror in the lid from an upright cathode ray tube.

OPPOSITE PAGE

TOP: Under the direction of Eustace Robb, (extreme r) a former guards officer, turned producer, an imaginative range of experimental 30-line programmes on the Baird system was broadcast by the BBC between 1932 and 1935. Among them was a boxing demonstration in August 1933. With the referee, managers and seconds were Laurie Raiterie and Archie Sexton.

BOTTOM LEFT: Charles Laughton was working on the comedy 'Vessel of Wrath' when he was interviewed at studios at Elstree in November 1937.

BOTTOM RIGHT ABOVE: Musical comedy stars, Cicely Courtneidge and Jack Hulbert, opened in 'Under Your Hat' at the Palace Theatre in November 1938. Interviewer, Tod Rich, spoke to them in the dressing room during an outside broadcast.

BOTTOM RIGHT BELOW: The Health Minister, Sir Kingsley Wood, talked about food and health in a programme in March 1937.

OVERLEAF:
The Radio Times with programmes for the first official week at Alexandra Palace. The billing for the opening was incorrect because the revised arrangements for the inauguration by the two television systems, Baird and Marconi-E.M.I. were too late for inclusion.

SHORT-WAVE—
VISION : 45 Mc/s
SOUND : 41.5 Mc/s

TELEVISION

> For two hours every day, except Sunday, programmes will be transmitted from Alexandra Palace, and details will be found on these pages each week. Apart from the historic interest of the opening ceremony, there are many outstanding items—Variety, dancing, star personalities, and a BBC film.
>
> ### THIS WEEK THE BAIRD SYSTEM WILL BE USED

Monday

3.0   Opening of the
BBC TELEVISION SERVICE
by
Major the Right Hon. G. C. TRYON,
M.P., H.M. Postmaster-General
Mr. R. C. NORMAN
(Chairman of the BBC)
and
the Right Hon. the Lord SELSDON,
K.B.E.
(Chairman of the Television
Advisory Committee)
will also speak

3.15   Interval
Time, Weather

3.20   BRITISH MOVIETONE NEWS

3.30   Variety
ADÈLE DIXON
Musical Comedy Star
BUCK AND BUBBLES
Comedians and Dancers
THE LAI FOUNS
Chinese Jugglers
THE BBC
TELEVISION ORCHESTRA
Leader, Boris Pecker
Conductor, HYAM GREENBAUM
Produced by DALLAS BOWER

Adèle Dixon is now playing lead opposite Laddie Cliff in the West End musical comedy *Over She Goes*. Amongst recent radio shows she has played in are *Lots of Love* and *Cottage Loaf*. Buck and Bubbles are a coloured pair who are now playing in *Transatlantic Rhythm*. They are versatile comedians who dance, play the piano, sing, and cross-chat. An Oriental juggling act, the Lai Founs consist of four men and two women who specialise in plate-spinning.

4.0   CLOSE
At the close of this afternoon's programme a chart arranged in co-operation with the Air Ministry will forecast the weather

9.0   PROGRAMME SUMMARY

9.5   'Television Comes to
London'
A BBC Film
In this film, specially taken for the BBC, viewers are given an idea of the growth of the television installation at Alexandra Palace and an insight into production routine. There will be many shots behind the scenes. One sequence, for instance, will show Adèle Dixon as she appears to viewers in the Variety at 3.30 this afternoon, and will then reveal the technical staff and equipment in the studio that made this transmission possible.

9.20   'Picture Page'
A Magazine of Topical and General
Interest
Devised and Edited by CECIL MADDEN
Produced by G. MORE O'FERRALL
The Switchboard Girl....JOAN MILLER

This is the first of a series in which people of interest will be introduced. In the recent test transmissions, Squadron-Leader Swain, who broke the aeroplane altitude record, was one of the subjects. In every way the technique is novel. For instance, Joan Miller, who links the show together, introduces each person by plugging in a telephone switchboard after a few preliminary words of description. She is a young Canadian actress who was recently leading lady in the Clemenceau play *The Tiger*, and last December she played in the radio version of *On the Spot*. Curiously enough, when she was in Vancouver she used to train telephone girls.

9.50   BRITISH MOVIETONE NEWS

10.0   CLOSE

Tuesday

3.0   PROGRAMME SUMMARY

3.5   ALSATIANS
A Display by Champion Alsatians from the Metropolitan and Essex Canine Society's Show
described by A. CROXTON SMITH, O.B.E.

3.15   BRITISH MOVIETONE NEWS

3.25   'THE GOLDEN HIND'
A model of Drake's famous ship made by L. A. STOCK, a Bus Driver, who will describe its construction

3.40   Interval
Time, Weather

3.45   Starlight
BEBE DANIELS and BEN LYON
The Hollywood Film Stars
In this series stars in every walk of life will appear. Bebe Daniels and Ben Lyon are names well-known to cinemagoers. One of Bebe Daniels's greatest successes was in *Rio Rita*, and in this act she may sing one or two numbers from it. Ben Lyon, her husband, has been in many outstanding film productions, such as *Hell's Angels* and *I Cover the Waterfront*.

4.0   CLOSE
At the close of this afternoon's programme a chart arranged in co-operation with the Air Ministry will forecast the weather

9.0   PROGRAMME SUMMARY

9.5   ALSATIANS
A Display by Champion Alsatians from the Metropolitan and Essex Canine Society's Show
described by A. CROXTON SMITH, O.B.E.

9.15   BRITISH MOVIETONE NEWS

9.25   'THE GOLDEN HIND'
A model of Drake's famous ship made by L. A. STOCK, a Bus Driver, who will describe its construction

9.40   Interval
Time, Weather

9.45   Starlight
MANUELA DEL RIO
In Spanish Dances, accompanied by Piano and Guitar

10.0   CLOSE

Wednesday

3.0   PROGRAMME SUMMARY

3.5   MARTIN TAUBMAN
with his Electronde
A Demonstration of its Music and
Effects
Most listeners of the pioneer days of radio will remember how the early sets were affected by objects brought close to them. The electronde is an instrument that turns these outside interferences to advantage. Martin Taubman will show viewers the extraordinary musical effects he can produce merely by a delicate motion of the hand. Ostensibly he is able to produce sound out of thin air.

3.20   BRITISH MOVIETONE NEWS

3.30   Interval
Time, Weather

3.35   THE BBC
DANCE ORCHESTRA
Directed by HENRY HALL
with
MOLLY, MARIE, and MARY
(The Three Sisters)
DAN DONOVAN
GEORGE ELRICK

4.0   CLOSE
At the close of this afternoon's programme a chart arranged in co-operation with the Air Ministry will forecast the weather

9.0   PROGRAMME SUMMARY

9.5   BRITISH MOVIETONE NEWS

The 'hello girl' of 'Picture Page'. This is Joan Miller, who will operate the switchboard for 'Picture Page', the first of which will be shown on Monday night at 9.20.

PROGRAMMES

9.15 Tempo and Taps

ROSALIND WADE
in a demonstration of Tap Dancing

Rosalind Wade, as well as being a brilliant dancer herself, has an extraordinary flair as a teacher. She has appeared in Variety and has organised dancing scenes in several Hollywood films. This, then, is a great chance for would-be tap-dancers to pick up a point or two from an expert.

Altogether, she runs eight dancing troupes. Radio listeners will remember the regular broadcasts of her Dancing Daughters.

9.35   Interval

Time, Weather

9.40 MARTIN TAUBMAN
with his Electronde

A Demonstration of its Music and Effects

10.0   CLOSE

Thursday

3.0 PROGRAMME SUMMARY

3.5 BRITISH MOVIETONE NEWS

3.15   Interval

Time, Weather

3.20 THE MERCURY BALLET

Marie Rambert's Company
in
Pavane and Tordion from Capriol Suite
(*Warlock. Choreography by Frederick Ashton*)

Solo from Swan Lake ⎫
Sugar Plum Fairy   ⎬ (*Tchaikovsky*)
Shepherd's Wooing
                  (*Handel, arr. Beecham*)
Solo from Foyer de Danse (*Berners*)
Columbine (*Tchaikovsky*)
La Golfeuse ⎫
Pompette   ⎬ (*Hugh Bradford*)
Pas de Trois from Alcina (*Handel*)
with
MAUDE LLOYD
WALTER GORE
ANDRÉE HOWARD
FRANK STAFF
HUGH LAING
THE BBC TELEVISION ORCHESTRA
Leader, Boris Pecker
Conductor, HYAM GREENBAUM

Marie Rambert was trained by Maestro Enrico Cecchetti, maître de ballet of the Diaghilev company. She appeared with that company in 1913, and later in London in the ballet *Pomme d'Or*. After her marriage to Ashley Dukes, she opened a school of ballet and founded the Ballet Club in her own little theatre now known as the Mercury. Here regular performances of ballet are given and a repertoire of over twenty-five original works has been produced. The company of young English choreographers and dancers trained by her includes Pearl Argyle, Maude Lloyd, Andrée Howard, Frederick Ashton, Harold Turner, Antony Tudor, William Chappell, and many others whose work has created an English tradition in ballet.

3.45 'Television Comes to London'
A BBC Film

4.0   CLOSE
At the close of this afternoon's programme a chart arranged in co-operation with the Air Ministry will forecast the weather

9.0 PROGRAMME SUMMARY

9.5 BRITISH MOVIETONE NEWS

9.15 Autumn Glory
Prize Chrysanthemums
from the National Chrysanthemum Society's Show
Described by W. WARDMAN and E. F. HAWES

9.30   Interval

Time, Weather

9.35 THE MERCURY BALLET
(*Details as at 3.20*)

10.0   CLOSE

Friday

3.0 PROGRAMME SUMMARY

3.5 Silver Fox Breeding
Four foxes will be exhibited by a representative of the Silver Fox Breeders' Association of Great Britain and Northern Ireland

3.20 BRITISH MOVIETONE NEWS

3.30   Interval

Time, Weather

3.35 From the London Theatre
SOPHIE STEWART
(*By permission of London Film Productions, Ltd.*)
in scenes from
The Royalty Theatre production
' Marigold '
a Scottish Comedy
by L. ALLEN HARKER and F. R. PRYOR
Stage Production by J. Graham Pockett and Lance Lister
with
Jean Clyde, Walter Roy, John Bailey, Brenda Harvey, Violet Moffat
Presentation by G. More O'Ferrall

Sophie Stewart, a Scot, made her first appearance in London in the title role of *Marigold* in 1929. She has played this part nearly a thousand times in England, Canada, and the United States since then, but this play had such a rare charm that it is once again revived in the West End.

Here you see Sophie Stewart (left) in the title rôle of *Marigold*, scenes from which will be broadcast on Friday afternoon at 3.35. With her are Jean Clyde as Mrs. Pringle and John Bailey as Forsyth.

4.0   CLOSE
At the close of this afternoon's programme a chart arranged in co-operation with the Air Ministry will forecast the weather

9.0 PROGRAMME SUMMARY

9.5 BRITISH MOVIETONE NEWS

9.15   Boxing
A Demonstration of Training
by Members of the
ALEXANDRA AMATEUR BOXING CLUB

9.35   Interval

Time, Weather

9.40 'Television Comes to London'
A BBC Film

10.0   CLOSE

Saturday

3.0 PROGRAMME SUMMARY

3.5 The Zoo Today
Some animals with their keepers
Introduced by DAVID SETH-SMITH

3.20 BRITISH MOVIETONE NEWS

3.30   Interval

Time, Weather

3.35   Cabaret
MABEL SCOTT
Singer of Modern Songs

HORACE KENNEY
Comedian

MOLLY PICON
In songs and impressions

THE BBC TELEVISION ORCHESTRA
Leader, Boris Pecker
Conductor, HYAM GREENBAUM
Production by DALLAS BOWER

4.0   CLOSE
At the close of this afternoon's programme a chart arranged in co-operation with the Air Ministry will forecast the weather

9.0 PROGRAMME SUMMARY

9.5 The Autumn Galleries
Pictures and Sculpture from Forthcoming Exhibitions
Described by JOHN PIPER

9.20 BRITISH MOVIETONE NEWS

9.30   Interval

Time, Weather

9.35   Cabaret
(*Details as at 3.35*)

10.0   CLOSE

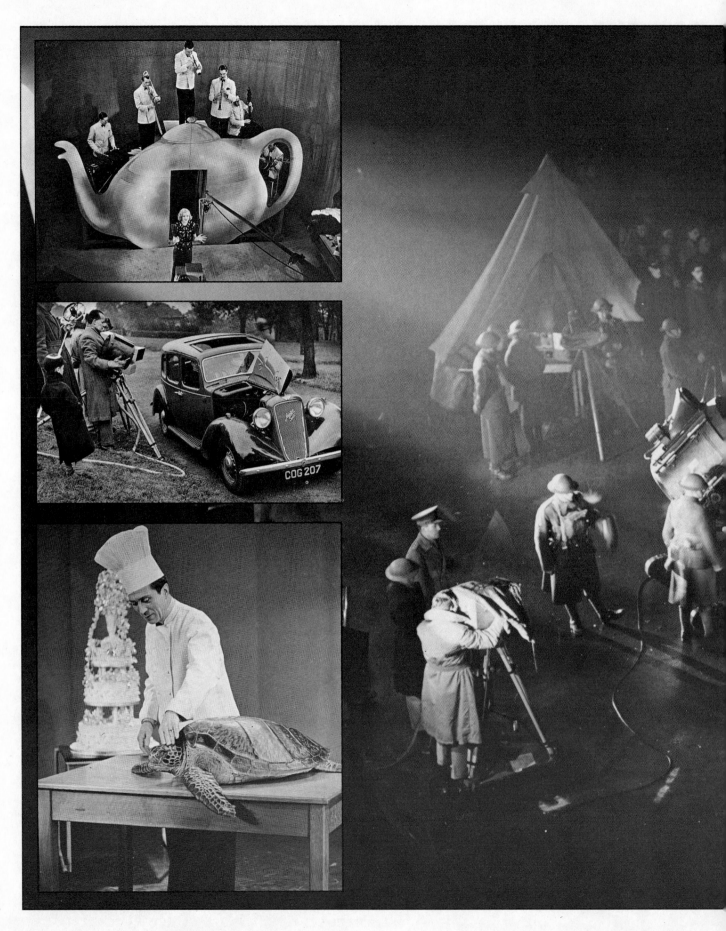

OPPOSITE PAGE

TOP: Eric Wilde and his Teatimers' group was formed from the main Television Orchestra (p 51) and it played on afternoon programmes. For this performance, 'Pastiche', the Teatimers backed the American actress, Claire Luce.

CENTRE: The art of the outside broadcast was still to be mastered, even with the mobile Emitron. The grounds of Alexandra Palace provided adequate opportunity for tests in October 1936. The car, at £235, was in the 1937 range of Austin Goodwoods being exhibited at the Motor Show at Olympia.

BOTTOM: Nouvelle cuisine was still more than 40 years away when television viewers were given a demonstration of art in the kitchen in January 1937. A French chef, a M. Dutrey, explained how to make a 'bandstand' of lobster shells. It is not clear from the records what artistic role the turtle played.

CENTRE SPREAD: That war might be approaching was reflected in a night-time outside broadcast in December 1936. Anti-aircraft equipment was brought to the terrace of Alexandra Palace so that local Territorial Army members could show their capabilities.

THIS PAGE

TOP: An afternoon performance of the one-act play 'How He Lied to Her Husband' in July 1937 was honoured by a visit from its author, George Bernard Shaw. At the end of the production he was invited to make 'on air' comments. With Shaw (centre) were (l to r) Greer Garson, Derek Williams, George More O'Ferrall (producer, on floor) and D.A. Clark-Smith.

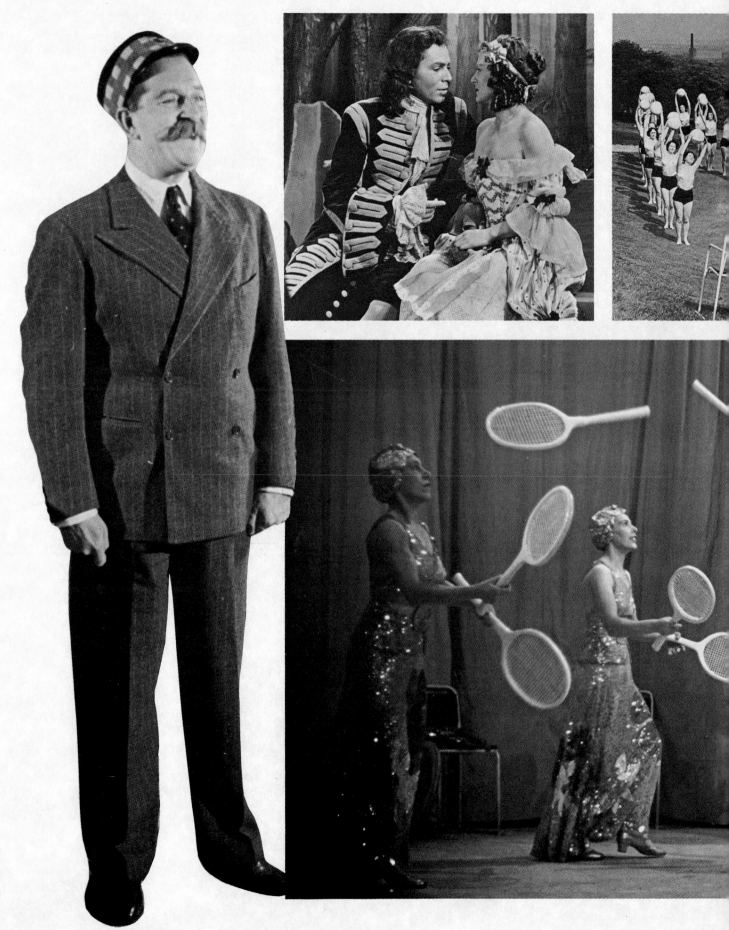

FAR LEFT: Stanley Holloway was no stranger to television having performed as a 30-line pioneer broadcaster in 1929. Ten years later he appeared in 'Cabaret' to deliver one of his famous monologues.

TOP LEFT: James Mason was a popular stage and film actor by 1939. In March he appeared in Moliere's 'L'Avare' with Majorie Mars.

TOP CENTRE: The Women's League of Health and Beauty was formed in 1930 'to enable business girls and busy women to improve their physique.' Classes, which exercised to music, took place throughout the country and in May 1937 there was a television demonstration in the grounds of Alexandra Palace. Earlier that year Prunella Stack, the daughter of the founder, is reported to have visited Germany to study methods of 'physical culture'.

THIS PAGE

TOP RIGHT: Jazz pianist, Fats Waller, was already a big name in the United States when he toured Britain in 1938. He featured in the 'Starlight' series in September.

BOTTOM CENTRE: 'The Five Carlton Sisters' in 'Cabaret' in June 1939.

THIS PAGE
In the pre-Alexandra Palace days, Christmas 1932 saw a performance of Dick Whittington (l to r) Ann Maitland (Dick); Fred Douglas (Cat); Betty Astell (Alice).

OPPOSITE PAGE

TOP LEFT: The Roehampton club, one of the country's top polo establishments, operated variations on a theme pre-war. Donkey polo was one, so was bicycle polo, televised in July 1939.

TOP RIGHT: Cabaret acts suitable for Ally Pally were regularly to be found in the major London hotels. One such was Nick Long junior, a tap dancer and his comedian partner, who were appearing at the Dorchester in September 1938. The comedian, who filled in between the dancing, was none other than Danny Kaye.

CENTRE: No, not a scene from an early Dr. Who, but a production of the fantasy play, R.U.R. (Rossum's Universal Robots) in February 1938. This classic, written in the twenties by Karel Capek, introduced the word 'robot' into the language. The cast included (l to r) Connaught Stanley, Derek Bond (robots); Larry Silverstone (Radius); Evan John, seated (Alquist).

BOTTOM: Following an introductory talk by the choreographer, Michel Fokine, the Russian Ballet performed an excerpt from 'Les Sylphides' in August 1938.

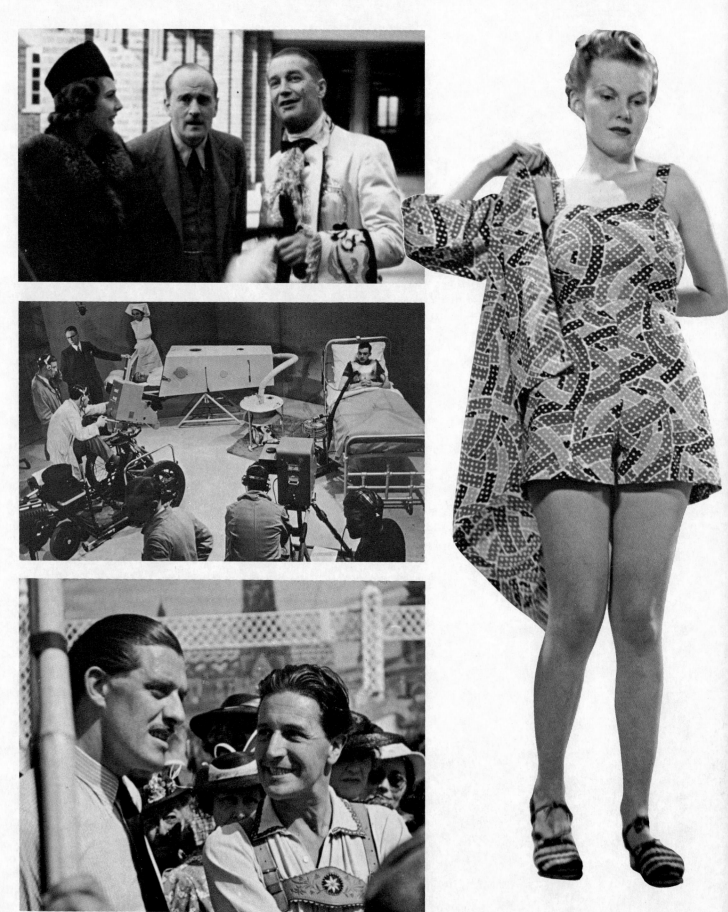

OPPOSITE PAGE

TOP LEFT: Maurice Chevalier (r) was making the costume comedy 'Break the News' at Pinewood studios with Jack Buchanan when he appeared on television in October 1937. Announcer, Elizabeth Cowell, interviewed him between takes. With them was Capt. the Hon. Richard Norton, Pinewood's managing director.

CENTRE: The iron lung (centre) and the cuirasse (r) were new methods of artificial respiration in the 1930s. They were demonstrated to viewers in December 1938.

BOTTOM: Ivor Novello was appearing in 'The Dancing Years' at Drury Lane when he attended a theatrical garden party in June 1939. Chatting to the lederhosen-clad star was the senior television announcer, Leslie Mitchell.

CUT OUT: The latest in swimwear was modelled in 'Informal Fashions' in June 1939.

THIS PAGE

TOP: The annual Radiolympia exhibition gave an opportunity for trial transmissions in the summer of 1936. The highlight was a revue, 'Here's Looking at You'. Singer, Helen McKay, performed the title song. With her, (l to r) were The Three Admirals (songs); Carol Chilton (Creole singer and dancer); Leslie Mitchell; Elizabeth Cowell; Maceo Thomas (with Carol Chilton); Helen McKay; The Griffiths Brothers (comedy horse) with 'Miss Lutie'.

BOTTOM: A May 1937 edition of the variety show 'Cabaret Cruise' was billed as fancy dress night. The cast included Dixon, saxophonist and Pal (the seal).

TOP: August 1932 marked the start of the BBC's control over 30-line productions broadcast by the Baird system. Transmissions got under way after a televised introduction by Baird himself. Viewers then saw (l to r) Louie Freear and Fred Douglas (musical comedy numbers); Betty Astell (songs) and Betty Bolton (songs and dances).

BOTTOM: The chimpanzees' tea party at London Zoo was an important part of the effort which went into boosting television at 1937's Radiolympia show, since fewer sets than expected had been sold. The BBC provided 90 promotional transmissions during the exhibition and Zoo tours were a regular ingredient.

OPPOSITE PAGE

TOP LEFT: Mr. George Swan was interviewed in September 1937 following his victory in a penny farthing cycle race. Supporting Mr. Swan and his trophy was Leslie Mitchell.

CENTRE: Margaret Lockwood returned from Hollywood in June 1939 where she had made 'Susannah of the Mounties' with Shirley Temple and Randolph Scott. Back in England, where she appeared on 'Picture Page' the same month, she was embarking on the comedy suspense film 'Night Train to Munich'.

RIGHT: Ray Milland and Ellen Drew were 'Picture Page' guests in April 1939 when they came over from the United States to make a screen version of the Terence Rattigan comedy, 'French Without Tears'.

BOTTOM: Dancers Ernest and Lotte Berk performed in 'Cafe Cosmopolitan' in February 1937. The general prohibition on advertising on the BBC dictated the appearance of a sign for Dubonnet as Bubonnet.

OPPOSITE PAGE

TOP LEFT: Richard Hearne had yet to become known as 'Mr. Pastry' to countless young viewers in the 1950s. But his slapstick comedy routines were well-established before the war as this sketch 'Bath – H. and C.' from October 1938 shows. In the bath was the film actress, Lilli Palmer. Looking on was George Nelson.

TOP RIGHT: When Leslie Mitchell interviewed him in October 1937, Primo Carnera was still a celebrity even though his career as a boxing champion had passed its peak. At 6ft 5¾ ins. and 19 stone, Carnera had been the heaviest world heavyweight title winner in history when he beat Jack Sharkey in 1933.

BOTTOM: Arthur Askey, at the piano, appeared in the variety programme, 'Do Help Yourselves' in October 1937. With him were (l to r) Marjorie Wynn-Hughes, Joyce Targett, Eleanor Fayre and Dudley Rolph.

THIS PAGE

TOP: The 'Television Follies' concert party appeared during a 20 minute interval in live coverage of Wimbledon in June 1937.

CENTRE: In October 1938 viewers were given a demonstration of how to deal with an incendiary bomb. That was in spite of the return of the Prime Minister, Neville Chamberlain, from his talks with Hitler and the promise of 'peace for our time', barely a month before.

BOTTOM: The presenter of 'Friends from the Zoo' David Seth-Smith (r) was in charge of birds and mammals at London Zoo. He had been a radio broadcaster since 1932 and had even given talks on experimental 30-line transmissions. Apart from showing penguins to viewers in December 1936 he had also taken a panda, a two-toed sloth and a blue and yellow macaw to Alexandra Palace.

TOP LEFT: Before the Trapp family was immortalised by Julie Andrews in 'The Sound of Music' the original Trapp choir from Saltzburg performed throughout pre-war Europe. They appeared on television in London in December 1937.

TOP RIGHT: Leslie Howard, the idol of the thirties and forties, was home from Hollywood in September 1937 when he appeared on 'Picture Page'. He was about to play Professor Higgins in 'Pygmalion' His role as Ashley Wilkes in 'Gone with the Wind' back in Hollywood was still 18 months away.

CENTRE: The outside broadcast cameras investigated life on the canals in March 1939. A Mr. and Mrs. Edwards were interviewed at Clitheroe's Lock on the Grand Union Canal by A.P. Herbert, the M.P. and writer.

CENTRE SPREAD: Bank Holiday, August 1939, the last month of peace before the outbreak of war, saw an outside broadcast camera in the children's pool at Finchley swimming baths in North London. With several hundred volts passing through the cables, bringing the viewers live entertainment was a risky business.

OPPOSITE PAGE

TOP: An integral part of the Alexandra Palace operation pre-war was the highly versatile television orchestra, seen in February 1937. The conductor was Hyam Greenbaum, an accomplished musician, who, at the age of sixteen had been a second violin under Henry Wood. The violinist (seated, second, l) was Eric Robinson who, after the war, himself became conductor of the Television Orchestra.

TOP: This typical room setting at the 1939 Radiolympia show was used to show off the latest model of a Philips television set. Prices by now had come down and this one was on sale at 35 guineas. Total sales had risen rapidly to about 20,000 but within a fortnight television had closed down for the war.

BOTTOM: A mainstay was the magazine programme 'Picture Page'. Canadian actress, Joan Miller, at a stage switchboard, introduced guests with the catchphrase 'You're through. You're looking at . . .' With her in 1936 was the production team and some guest including (l of switchboard) Prince Monolulu, the tipster, Dinah Sheridan, then a poster model and Leslie Mitchell who conducted most interviews

THE FORTIES

After a wartime break of almost seven years the television service resumed in June 1946. Programmes began on June 7th; but the main reopening event was the outside broadcast of the Victory Parade the following day. It is estimated that up to 100,000 viewers watched as the Royal Family took the salute in The Mall.

As Leslie Mitchell, Elizabeth Cowell and Jasmine Bligh had become well-known before the war, so three new announcers rose to prominence when television re-started. They were (top l) Sylvia Peters who was appointed in 1947 after wartime stage experience; McDonald Hobley, who joined in 1946 after war service and a pre-war acting career; Mary Malcolm, who had been a wartime radio announcer and who went to Alexandra Palace in 1948.

TOP: The then Princess Elizabeth and the Duke of Edinburgh paid an informal visit to Alexandra Palace in July 1948. The Prince and Princess, said to be keen viewers, saw a variety show, 'Hulbert's Follies', being transmitted and afterwards spoke to Jack Hulbert (next to Prince Philip) and to Alexandra Palace staff.

CENTRE: The Windmill Girls took part in a test broadcast from Alexandra Palace in April 1946 as plans were made for the official reopening.

BOTTOM: A starring role in 'The Avengers' series for Patrick Macnee was still about 15 years away when he appeared as a Russian officer in Shaw's 'Arms and the Man' in December 1946.

OPPOSITE PAGE
Joan Gilbert had been involved behind the scenes with 'Picture Page' since its pre-war days. When the programme restarted in 1946 she became its editor and presenter. As television spread beyond London she enjoyed a large following for what was described as her 'unpredictable effervescence'.

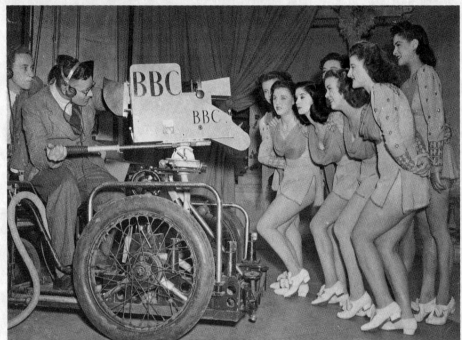

The Beverley Sisters, Joy and twins, Babs and Teddie, had made a name for themselves on the radio when they were booked for one of the first post-war programmes, an edition of 'Cabaret Cruise' in July 1946.

TOP: The outside broadcast cameras went to the wartime fighter base, North Weald aerodrome north of London, during Battle of Britain week in September 1949. Flanked by a Mk. 16 Spitfire from 1943, Richard Dimbleby talked to three Battle of Britain pilots including (r) the legendary Group Captain Douglas Bader.

BOTTOM: Actress, Anna Neagle, was an occasional guest on 'Television Dancing Club'. With her, in a March 1949 programme, was Victor Sylvester, who provided the music with his ballroom orchestra.

OPPOSITE PAGE

Norman Wisdom was given his own television show 'Wit and Wisdom' in the autumn of 1948 coinciding with his overnight success in the 'International Variety Season' at the London Casino the same year.

INSET: In an 'At the Zoo' outside broadcast in July 1949 one of the guests of presenter Richard Dimbleby (p 71) was Spike, the Orang Utang.

OPPOSITE PAGE

TOP LEFT: George Cole (l) and Alastair Sim appeared in January 1949 in 'The Anatomist', a play about the Edinburgh body snatchers, Burke and Hare.

BOTTOM LEFT: 'Jolly', the equilibrist was one of the turns in a July 1948 edition of the cabaret show, 'Cafe Continental'.

RIGHT: Edward Molyneux, although British-born, had been a top fashion designer in Paris for more than 25 years when he exhibited his latest collection on the programme 'Haute Couture de Paris' in April 1949. The model was wearing 'a morning-into-afternoon' suit.

THIS PAGE

TOP LEFT: Eleven-year old King Feisal of Iraq was a 'Picture Page' guest in 1946. The English-educated king acceded to the throne at the age of four. He was assassinated in a coup in 1958 after which Iraq became a republic.

TOP RIGHT: One of Joan Gilbert's 'Picture Page' guests in February 1948 was boxer, Freddie Mills. He had just retained his European cruiser-weight title in a fight with the Spaniard, Pago Bueno.

CENTRE: Philip Harben had been the experimental kitchen supervisor to British Overseas Airways when he joined television in 1946. As the television cook he advised viewers on 'Your Christmas Dinner' in 1949. Joan Gilbert and her guests, who included a bus conductor and a nurse, sampled the results of his studio efforts.

BOTTOM: Man-made fibres were still novel enough in May 1949 to devote a programme to fashion clothes made from rayon. This sportswear was part of a range of clothes modelled.

TOP: 'At Home Abroad' tried to give viewers an idea of other cultures. An edition of July 1947 looked at life in China. Clearly, it was not possible to film on location so in this, as in other cases, a set was built at Alexandra Palace.

BOTTOM: 'The Gentle People', an anti-fascist allegory, made television history in May 1949. Most of the action took place at or near a New York waterfront. Normally this would have meant location filming; but the result would have been more a cinema than a television production. So a water tank was installed in the studio, a feat never before attempted. Special effects gave the impression of waves and of the dinghy moving.
The jetty was hinged to give a bigger expanse of water to represent mid-harbour scenes. (l to r) Robert Ayres (the gangster); Macdonald Park (Magruder, the policeman); Abraham Sofaer (Jonah Goodman); Ernest Jay (Philip Anagnos).

OPPOSITE PAGE

TOP LEFT: Harry Secombe had yet to achieve national recognition as a Goon when he sang in 'Rooftop Rendezvous' in November 1948. The show was a rival to 'Cafe Continental' and included such attractions as Jack Jackson and the Rendezvous Orchestra and the Rooftop Lovelies.

TOP RIGHT: J.B. Priestley was the first contributor in November 1949 to a new series, 'Personal Impressions'.

BOTTOM: Christmas 1946 saw a production of 'Alice in Wonderland'. (l to r) Philip Stainton (the Mock Turtle); Vivien Pickles (Alice); and Hilary Pritchard (Gryphon).

TOP: Some of the stars of children's television paraded themselves before a young viewer in February 1948. (l to r) Oswald the Ostrich, Muffin the Mule, Wolly the Gog and Mr. Peregrine the Penguin. Absent on that occasion was Wolly's better half, Molly.

CENTRE: Muffin the Mule was the first television character to become a national children's favourite. With Annette Mills and the puppetry, generally, of Ann Hogarth, Muffin first appeared in October 1946.

BOTTOM: Jennifer Gay was billed as the first schoolgirl to announce children's television programmes. She took up her duties at the age of 14 in 1949. After three years she left to pursue a career in ballet.

Televising the Coronation in June 1953 was the biggest event in broadcasting history, both radio and television, to date. Apart from the 20 million who saw the six and half hours of the procession and ceremony live in this country about 257 million more saw it, either live or filmed, in Europe and North America. Temporary transmitters were installed in parts of Britain not yet able to receive programmes. Television sets sold as never before and 3,000 tickets for a large-screen showing at the Festival Hall went within an hour. Unlike the 1937 Coronation, cameras were allowed inside Westminster Abbey as well as throughout the route of the procession.

OPPOSITE PAGE
TOP LEFT: The State Coach passed Victoria Embankment on the way to Westminster Abbey.

TOP RIGHT: The Queen as she appeared on television screens.

THIS PAGE
TOP LEFT: The Queen and the Duke of Edinburgh on the Buckingham Palace balcony after the Coronation.

TOP RIGHT: Richard Dimbleby, in his Coronation commentary box. His name was to become synonymous with commentaries on all great state occasions. He was originally appointed a BBC 'news observer', a job which he suggested to the Corporation himself. After covering major events pre-war and travelling more than 100,000 miles as a war correspondent he joined television where he hosted countless programmes. He became anchor man for Panorama in 1957.

CENTRE SPREAD: Viewers saw this Coronation firework display on Thames Side at Westminister.

TOP: The twelve 'Television Toppers' made BBC history in 1953 by each winning contracts worth £1,000 a year. These 'Toppers' were in the 'class' of September 1959.

BOTTOM: The comedian and conductor, Vic Oliver, had his own series, 'This is Show Business'. His guest in a September 1952 programme was actress, Zsa Zsa Gabor.

OPPOSITE PAGE

TOP LEFT: Comedian, Terry-Thomas, like so many of his contemporaries first performed on radio and in cabaret before moving to television. In this sketch from his series 'How Do You View?' in December 1950 he appeared with Avril Angers.

TOP RIGHT: Bernard Braden and Barbara Kelly came to England from their native Canada in 1949 and were in a range of television and radio comedy, drama and variety programmes. In 1953 Barbara Kelly was a panel member of 'What's My Line?'. In July the same year they both appeared in a television version of their radio show 'Barbara with Braden.'

BOTTOM: 'Television Dancing Club' started in 1948. In a November 1950 edition, competitors danced the tango to the music of Victor Sylvester's ballroom orchestra.

TOP LEFT: The General Election in February 1950 was the first covered on television. Computer graphics were unheard of and party progress was charted by hand. The pundits (l to r) were David Butler, research fellow at Nuffield College and R.B. McCallum a fellow academic. Chester Wilmot (r) an experienced broadcaster was anchorman. Labour won by a narrow margin.

STAR: After training at the Royal Academy of Dramatic Art, Diana Dors was contracted to the Rank Organisation. She appeared in numerous films and television series. Her first television acting role was in a drama, 'Face to Face' in January 1951, in which she played half of a song and dance double act.

TOP RIGHT: Robert Dougall joined the BBC in 1934 as a radio announcer on the Overseas Service. After the war he resumed his announcing work and also became one of a panel of television and radio newsreaders. This picture was taken in 1956.

BOTTOM: The Grove Family soap opera ran from 1953 to 1956. In a scene from an April 1954 episode were (l to r) Nancy Roberts (Grandma); Sheila Sweet (Pat); Ruth Dunning (Mrs. Grove); Edward Evans (Mr. Grove); Christopher Beeny (Lennie); Andrew Leigh (Mr. Cutler) and Margaret Downs (Daphne).

THIS PAGE

Tommy Cooper's career was going from strength to strength when he appeared in the television Christmas Party from Alexandra Palace in 1952. He had had his London Palladium debut that summer and had gone on tour with the show 'Television Highlights'. Acting as his straight man for a trick was announcer, McDonald Hobley.

CENTRE: In October 1950 designers were indulging themselves in the luxury of using vast amounts of material, still in short supply because of post war austerity. Viewers' appetites were whetted in 'Paris Fashion'.

TOP LEFT: Alma Cogan had more than 20 hits before her premature death in 1966. She reached number one in May 1955 with 'Dreamboat' and just after the release of 'Whatever Lola Wants' in March 1957 she starred in her own television series. Her guest of the week in April was Harry Secombe who played 'Napoleon' to her 'Josephine'.

TOP RIGHT: Patrick Troughton, later to become a 'Doctor Who', appeared in the title role in 'Robin Hood' in 1953.

BOTTOM: Wilfred Pickles started life as a builder but became a radio broadcaster in 1931. In the 1940s and early 1950s he had regular radio series and also appeared on the stage. Among his television shows was 'Ask Pickles', a similar format to 'Jim'll Fix It'. With him in a December 1954 edition were ex-Tiller Girls and pilots of 92 Squadron R.A.F.

THIS PAGE

TOP: Kenneth Williams (l) appeared in the Shaw comedy, 'Misalliance' in July 1954, playing Bentley Summerhays. With him was Richard Leech as Johnny Tarleton.

BOTTOM: 'The Black and White Minstrel Show' was still four years away when 'The Minstrel Show' appeared on children's television in July 1954.

THIS PAGE

TOP: Arthur Askey's television career started in the 30-line days. In 'Before Your Very Eyes' in April 1952 he went through a routine with straight man, Jerry Desmonde.

BOTTOM: In 1950, at the age of 18, Petula Clark (r) became 'Woman Television Personality of the Year'. In 1952 she had her own television series 'Pet's Parlour'. In a February programme her guests were (l to r) Joe Henderson, her accompanist; Denis Goodwin, comedian and scriptwriter; her sister, Barbara; Bob Monkhouse, comedian and scriptwriter.

OPPOSITE PAGE

TOP: 'What's My Line?' with Eamonn Andrews as chairman began in 1951. A panel of four had to guess the occupations of a number of challengers such as that of the man who was a saggar maker's bottom knocker in the pottery industry. The best-known panellist was the irascible and outspoken Gilbert Harding. The other team members in a June 1952 edition were (l to r) Marghanita Laski, Jerry Desmonde and Elizabeth Allan.

BOTTOM LEFT: In October 1951 Somerset Maugham was interviewed about his portrait which Graham Sutherland had recently completed.

BOTTOM RIGHT TOP: A 'Picture Page' guest in June 1950 was Geoffrey Duke, a 27-year-old Birmingham motor mechanic. He had won the senior international Isle of Man T.T. race with a record speed of 92.27 m.p.h. The interviewer was Graham Walker, editor of 'Motor Cycling'.

BOTTOM RIGHT: Frankie Howerd had become established on the radio when he moved into television where he had a series 'The Howerd Crowd'. With him in a sketch in January 1952 was character actor, Victor Platt.

What's my Line?

CENTRE SPREAD: Daphne Slater (l) with Prunella Scales, who was two decades away from 'Fawlty Towers', appeared respectively as Georgina Seymour and Prudence Buckland in a March 1954 production of the historical romance, 'Beau Brummell'.

INSET: Julie Andrews aged 19, had been an actress for six years when she appeared in 'Limelight' in September 1954. As a child star she had already appeared in a Royal Command Performance and had become well-known to radio audiences as 'Archie's' playmate in 'Educating Archie', with ventriloquist, Peter Brough. She left for the United States later in 1954 and went on to become an international star after her first film, 'Mary Poppins' in 1963.

TOP: When 'Tonight' started in February 1957 it took a down to earth approach to television journalism, covering the serious and the bizarre. (l to r) Donald Baverstock (producer); Cy Grant (singer and guitarist who often signed the programme off); Janette Fairer (secretary); Cliff Michelmore (anchorman); Jonathan Miller (guest artist).

CENTRE LEFT: 'The Quatermass Experiment', transmitted in 1953 was the first sci-fi series to have audiences glued to their seats. In the opening episode were (l to r) Reginald Tate, Duncan Lamont (the astronaut); Moray Watson; W. Thorpe Devereux; Paul Witsun Jones and Isabel Dean.

CIRCLE: Walt Disney was a 'Picture Page' guest in June 1951. Most of the film industry refused to let films be televised fearing that cinema attendances would slump. Walt Disney was an exception in allowing his cartoons to be shown.

CENTRE RIGHT: 'Six Five Special' the first teenage pop show began in in February 1957. With Peter Murray (l) and Josephine Douglas in an early edition was Lonnie Donegan.

BOTTOM: 'Inventors Club' started in 1948 to try to stimulate ideas. A range of inventions appeared including this multi-cake icer in October 1951.

THIS PAGE

TOP: Donald Peers 'the Cavalier of Song' was a heartthrob in the 1940s and 1950s. He went to television with 'the Donald Peers Show' from which this was a scene in a January 1952 programme.

BOTTOM: When 'This is Your Life' with Eamonn Andrews started in July 1955, the BBC had reservations that its audience would not approve of the intrusion into people's private lives. Vera Lynn was the subject in October 1957.

TOP: The distinctly unacademic activities at Chiselbury school arrived on the screen in October 1956. The 'Whack-o' team in this 1959 episode was led, as ever, by headmaster 'Professor' Jimmy Edwards with his assistant, Mr. Pettigrew, played by Arthur Howard.

BOTTOM: Blue Peter made its first appearance in October 1958 and has been going ever since. Its first presenters were Christopher Trace, a 25-year old ex-Army officer turned actor, and Leila Williams, 21, who was Miss Great Britain, 1957.

OPPOSITE PAGE

TOP LEFT: Richard Hearne, who had appeared on television pre-war was established by 1950 as a children's favourite in his role as Mr Pastry. He was in characteristic garb in a New Year's Eve edition of 'Mr. Pastry's Progress'.

TOP RIGHT: Cliff Michelmore started his broadcasting career with the British Forces Network and also became well-known for 'Two Way Family Favourites'. Before becoming anchorman in 'Tonight' he was involved in a number of television programmes in the early 50s including 'Telescope' for children. With him in May 1951 was Elizabeth Cruft, great granddaughter of the dog-show founder, in an item, 'Your Puppy'.

BOTTOM: The author of the 'Billy Bunter' stories, Frank Richards, wrote special versions for the television series which started in 1952. With Billy Bunter, centre, played by Gerald Campion were (l to r) Brian Smith (Bob Cherry); Harry Searle (Harry Wharton); Barry MacGregor (John Bull); Michael Danvers-Walker (Frank Nugent); Ronald Moody (Hurree Singh).

84

OPPOSITE PAGE

TOP: An addition to the children's programme 'family' was the 'Woodentops' whose adventures were first recounted in September 1955.

CENTRE: Valerie Hobson had appeared in a number of films and on the stage when she became a presenter of 'Telescope'. With her in a December 1950 edition were 'Timothy Telescope' and 'Cactus the Camel'.

BOTTOM: Bill and Ben, the Flowerpot Men, not forgetting Little Weed, joined the children's programme schedules in December 1952. The 'identical twins' were manipulated by puppeteers, Audrey Atterbury and Molly Gibson.

THIS PAGE

TOP: Another children's favourite were 'The Little Grey Rabbit' stories by Alison Uttley. They were told by Jan Bussell and Ann Hogarth with their glove puppets. This was a scene in an October 1950 edition.

BOTTOM: Prudence Kitten was another of Annette Mills' puppet creations for children and who came to the screen in March 1951.

TOP: The opening of the transmitter at Holme Moss near Manchester in October 1951 brought television to the north of England. Among guests at the opening ceremony was the 'Wizard of the Dribble' Stanley Matthews, who was introduced to the technicalities of the television camera by Richard Dimbleby.

BOTTOM: Following the opening of the Kirk O'Shotts transmitter in March 1952, bringing television to southern Scotland, 'Music Hall' was first televised from the Metropole Theatre in Glasgow in November that year. Centre stage for the 'Pageant of Scotland' finale was Gracie Fields.

TOP: For the first time, in June 1968, viewers were able to see the 'Trooping the Colour' ceremony in colour. The full colour service started officially on BBC 2 the previous December and in the first nine months of 1968 more than 100,000 colour sets were sold.

CENTRE LEFT: The highly-acclaimed film 'Royal Family' first televised in June 1969, marked a new phase not only in the view it gave the public of the monarchy, but also in the media's approach to royal coverage.

CENTRE RIGHT: The 'Dad's Army' comedy series took as its theme the war time Local Defence Volunteers (later the Home Guard). The series which started in July 1968 starred (l to r) Arnold Ridley (Pte. Godfrey); Clive Dunn (L/Cpl Jones); Arthur Lowe (Capt. Mainwaring); Ian Lavender (Pte. Pike); John Laurie (Pte. Frazer); John Le Mesurier Sgt. Wilson).

BOTTOM: There was special coverage of the Apollo moon-flights in the late 1960s and in the early hours of July 21st 1969 viewers saw live pictures of man's first steps on the moon. Transmissions were in black and white; but this picture was taken on the lunar surface.

OPPOSITE PAGE

One of the most memorable series of the 1960s was 'Civilisation'. Beginning in February 1969, the distinguished art historian and critic, Sir Kenneth Clark, examined the ideas and values which gave meaning to the term 'Western Civilisation'. His quest took him to the Celtic Hebrides and to many other parts of the world.

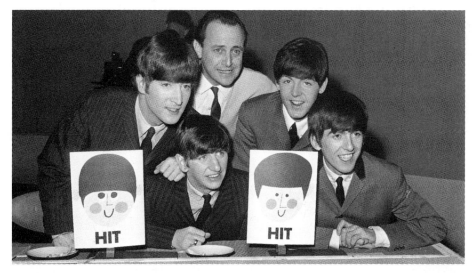

OPPOSITE PAGE
'The Man from Uncle', the light-hearted spy adventures of the team from United Network Command for Law Enforcement had their British debut in June 1965. The main characters were (l to r) David McCallum (Ilya Kuryiakin); Robert Vaughn (Napoleon Solo); Leo G. Carroll (Alexander Waverly).

THIS PAGE

TOP: 'Juke Box Jury', in which verdicts on the latest releases were announced by either a klaxon for a miss or a bell for a hit, began in June 1959. With its chairman, David Jacobs, the programme was transmitted from Liverpool in December 1963 with the Beatles as 'jurors' (l to r) John Lennon, Ringo Starr, David Jacobs, Paul McCartney and George Harrison. Their record 'I Want to Hold Your Hand', reached number one in the hit parade the same month.

CENTRE: Bandleader, Billy Cotton called 'Wakey Wakey' for the 'Billy Cotton Bandshow' for the first time on television in March 1956, With Billy Cotton (centre) for the 'Any Old Iron' finale from an October 1963 show were (l to r) Renato Rascel, Russ Conway and Jimmy James.

BOTTOM: 'It's a Square World' and its particular brand of lunacy held centre stage for comedy in the early 1960s. In 1963 it was entered for the Golden Rose of Montreux award; but while it did not win it was awarded the prestigious International Press Prize. Michael Bentine, a former 'Goon Show' star (l) was the front man and with him was Frank Thornton who has appeared in countless comedy shows.

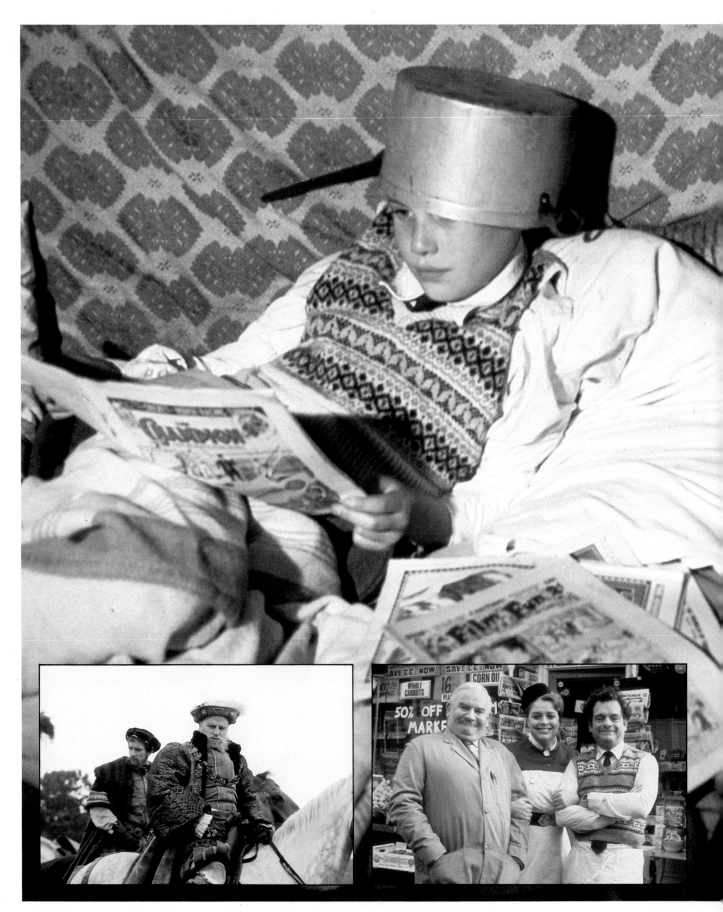

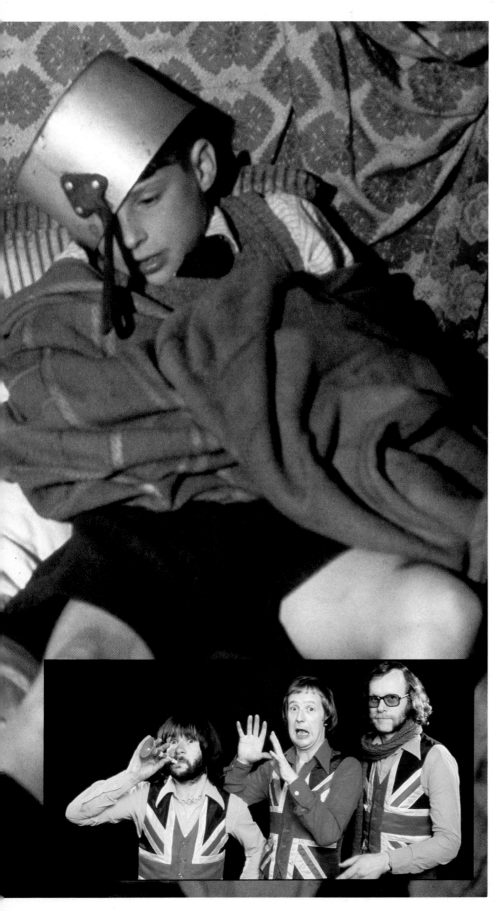

CENTRE SPREAD: 'The Evacuees' broadcast in March 1975 was a dramatised account of the evacuation of two Jewish boys from Manchester during the war. It starred (l to r) Steven Serember (Neville) and Gary Carp (Danny).

OPPOSITE PAGE
BOTTOM LEFT: Keith Michell starred as Henry VIII in 'The Six Wives of Henry VIII' which started its run in January 1970. John Ronane played Thomas Seymour.

BOTTOM RIGHT: 'Open All Hours' stars (l to r) Ronnie Barker as 'Arkwright' the stuttering grocer, permanently engaged to Nurse Gladys Emmanuel, played by Lynda Baron and David Jason as his put-upon nephew, Granville. The comedy series began in February 1976.

THIS PAGE
The 'Goodies' comedy team arrived on the scene in November 1970. (l to r) Bill Oddie, Tim Brooke-Taylor, Graeme Garden.

TOP: 'Dr. Finlay's Casebook', started in August 1962 and charted events in a Scottish rural practice in the 1920s. It starred (l to r) Andrew Cruickshank (Dr. Cameron); Barbara Mullen (Janet); Bill Simpson (Dr. Finlay).

BOTTOM: 'Cathy Come Home', televised in May 1966, dealt with the plight of homeless young mothers and helped to end the policy of separating homeless husbands and their families. It starred (l to r) Sean King (Sean); Ray Brooks (Ray); Stephen King (Stephen); Carol White (Cathy).

OPPOSITE PAGE

TOP: 'The Forsyte Saga' began on BBC-2 in January 1967. The Forsyte family, whose fortunes were chronicled, comprised (l to r) (back) Cyril Luckham (Sir Lawrence Mont); Nicholas Pennel (Michael Mont); Eric Porter (Soames Forsyte); Martin Jarvis (Jon); Jonathan Burn (Val). (Front) June Barry (June); Margaret Tyzack (Winifred); Susan Hampshire (Fleur); Karen Fernald (Anne); Nyree Dawn Porter (Irene); Suzanne Neve (Holly).

CENTRE LEFT: Huw Wheldon (second l) started the arts magazine 'Monitor' in 1958. An October 1963 edition discussed 'Hamlet'. Taking part were Peter O'Toole (back to camera) who was appearing in the role at the National Theatre, Orson Welles and Ernest Milton a Hamlet of the 1920s. Huw Wheldon was Managing Director of BBC Television from 1969-75.

BOTTOM LEFT: One of the best-known of the Hancock's Half Hour comedy shows starring Tony Hancock, was 'The Blood Donor' seen in June 1961. With him were Frank Thornton and June Whitfield.

BOTTOM RIGHT: Gerald Harper played 'Adam Adamant', a Victorian superman, kept in suspended animation for over 60 years. In the 1966 series Juliet Harmer played his assistant Georgina Jones.

THIS PAGE: 'Fawlty Towers' first appeared in September 1975. The comedy starred John Cleese as the manic Torquay hotelier Basil Fawlty and Prunella Scales as his long-suffering but shrewish wife, Sybil.

CENTRE SPREAD
'Telford's Change', starting in January 1979, starred Peter Barkworth as Mark Telford and Hannah Gordon as his wife, Sylvia. It was the story of the couple's efforts to reconcile their ambitions with the practical demands of their lives.

OPPOSITE PAGE
TOP: Part of the 'Monty Python's Flying Circus' team in customarily bizarre poses in a 1970 instalment.

CENTRE: 'Steptoe and Son' the comedy starring Harry H. Corbett as Harold and Wilfred Brambell as his grubby father was first broadcast in 1962. Harold's description of his father as 'You dirty old man' became a catch phrase. This scene was in a 1974 episode.

BOTTOM: Comedian, Dick Emery, seen here in a typical role in 1979, was famous for his catch phrase 'Ooh, you are awful'. He began his BBC television appearances in October 1965.

OPPOSITE PAGE

TOP LEFT: More than nine million tuned in on Saturday nights in 1962-3 to watch 'That Was The Week That Was'. With (l to r) David Frost, William Rushton, Millicent Martin, Roy Kinnear, Lance Percival et al, it set new standards in television satire and became synonymous with the swinging sixties.

CENTRE LEFT: 'Z-Cars' revolutionised crime series on British television. Its realistic approach to police work contrasted sharply with the homely 'Dixon of Dock Green'. In an October 1963 'Z-Cars' episode were (l to r) James Ellis (PC Herbert Lynch); Colin Welland (PC David Graham); Joseph Brady (PC Jock Weir); Brian Blessed (PC 'Fancy' Smith).

TOP RIGHT: Harry Worth first appeared on television in 1947 as a ventriloquist. He starred in several comedy series playing the affable buffoon. This was a scene from an October 1968 episode.

CENTRE: Rodney Bewes (l) as 'Bob' and James Bolam as 'Terry' were the 'Likely Lads'. The comedy series, about two incident-prone Northeasterners, began its run in December 1964.

BOTTOM: 'Till Death Us Do Part' caused enormous controversy when it started, largely because of the language. But it was highly successful. The first series began in June 1966 and centred on the bigoted Alf Garnett (Warren Mitchell) (l). His family comprised his layabout son-in-law, Mike (Anthony Booth); his daughter, Mike's wife, Rita, (Una Stubbs) and his wife, Elsie, referred to by Garnett as 'Silly Moo', played by Dandy Nichols.

THIS PAGE

'Compact', a soap opera set on a women's magazine, ran for three years from 1962. Ronald Allen played the editor, Ian Harman.

OPPOSITE PAGE
Comedians Ronnie Barker (r) and Ronnie Corbett teamed up as 'The Two Ronnies' in 1971.

THIS PAGE

TOP LEFT: Sir David Attenborough has become famous for his wild-life films and has presented numerous series. 'Life on Earth' began in 1979, from which this was a scene.

TOP RIGHT: Since 'Jim'll Fix It' started in May 1975 about two and a half million hopefuls have written to Jimmy Savile hoping that he can make their dearest wishes come true.

BOTTOM: Larry Grayson, with Isla St. Clair, took over the 'Generation Game' family competition show from Bruce Forsyth in September 1978.

TOP LEFT: Larry Hagman as J.R. Ewing in the highly successful soap opera about the often troubled but always rich lives of the Ewing clan in 'Dallas'. Since the series started in September 1978, the ruthless and scheming J.R. has become almost a cult figure – the man you love to hate.

BOTTOM: The long-running children's programme 'Blue Peter' went to Kenya with Princess Anne in April 1971 to make the special film 'Blue Peter Royal Safari'. With the Princess was presenter, Valerie Singleton.

OPPOSITE PAGE

TOP RIGHT: The Royal Wedding of the Prince of Wales and Lady Diana Spencer in July 1981 was the biggest broadcasting event undertaken. Almost a quarter of the world's population either saw it on television or listened to it. Sixty BBC television cameras were used. The Coronation of George VI 44 years earlier had used a mere three.

CENTRE: The lavishly produced soap opera about the hugely wealthy and consistently distraught Carrington family of Denver arrived on television screens in May 1982 in the form of 'Dynasty'. It stars (l ro r) Joan Collins (Alexis Carrington Colby (l)); John Forsythe (Blake Carrington); Linda Evans (Krystle Carrington).

BOTTOM: When 'Breakfast Time' started in January 1983 it made television history as the first networked breakfast show in Europe. The presentation team's celebrations after the successful launch involved (l to r) (back) Francis Wilson, Nick Ross, David Icke, (front) Barbara Walters, presenter of a United States breakfast show and a 'Breakfast Time' guest, Debbie Rix, Frank Bough, Selina Scott and Russell Grant.

TOP LEFT: 'That's Life' with Esther Rantzen's inimitable approach to consumer affairs began in May 1973. With her in a January 1976 edition were (l to r) Kieran Prendiville and Glyn Worsnip.

BELOW: Harry Corbett returned to the screen with a new series of 'Sooty' stories in September 1965. With Sooty was 'Soo'.

CENTRE: Few series have been as successful as 'Dr. Who' in sustaining enthusiastic support over more than two decades. The Doctor, described as an ageless guardian of galactic peace came into view in November 1963 and over the years seven actors have played the television title role. Each has had to pit the Doctor's wits against a string of enemies including Cybermen, Zarbi, Silurians and Krotons. But the most famous of Dr. Who's adversaries will always be the Daleks who made their debut opposite the first Dr. Who, William Hartnell, in December 1963.

BOTTOM: The diametrically opposite life-styles of the Goods and the Leadbeatters was the basis of 'The Good Life' comedy series which began in April 1975. Barbara and Tom Good, played by Felicity Kendal and Richard Briers (l) opted out of the rat race and converted their garden into a small-holding. But their well-heeled neighbours, Jerry and Margo Leadbeatter, played by Paul Eddington and Penelope Keith, thrived on the stresses and strains of the consumer society.

OPPOSITE PAGE

Disc-jockey, Simon Dee, hosted his own chat show, 'Dee-Time' for a period from April 1967. He also took part in a number of pop music programmes.

CENTRE SPREAD
Up to six live reports a day were
broadcast from the Los Angeles
Olympic Games in 1984. As with
previous Games satellite links were
crucial to the coverage.

OPPOSITE PAGE
TOP: Billed as the 'department store
of the air', 'Saturday Superstore'
began in October 1982 offering a
miscellany of music, star guest
spots, items of interest and general
fun for younger viewers. At the
counter, (l to r) presenters Sarah
Greene, Keith Chegwin and Mike
Read.

CENTRE: Holiday camp life in the
1950s is the basis for the comedy
'Hi De Hi' starring Paul Shane as
Ted Bovis the wheeler-dealer camp
host and Su Pollard as Peggy the
scatterbrained chalet maid. The
series started in February 1981.

TOP INSET: Dr. Jacob Bronowski presented a series of 13 programmes filmed all over the world in which he gave his personal view of the evolution of scientific thought. 'The Ascent of Man' began its run in November 1973.

BOTTOM INSET: Derek Jacobi starred in the title role in the award-winning series 'I Claudius'. The 12-part adaptation of novels by Robert Graves started its run in 1976 and has recently been repeated.

CENTRE SPREAD

Nicola Pagett starred in the title role of Anna Karenina in the television adaptation of the Tolstoy novel. The ten part serialisation began in September 1977.

THIS PAGE

TOP: For more than a decade, 'Last of the Summer Wine' has chronicled the lives of three old codgers with time on their hands in and around a small Yorkshire town. Its gentle humour has taken it to the top of the ratings. In customary pose in a 1979 episode were (l to r) Bill Owen (Compo); Brian Wilde (Foggy); Peter Sallis (Clegg).

CENTRE: Ronnie Barker (centre) as the cunning but likeable jail bird, Fletcher was the star of 'Porridge' set in the imaginary Slade prison. His cellmate (r) was Godber played by Richard Beckinsale, while offering an unfriendly word of advice in a 1975 edition was Prison Officer Mackay, played by Fulton Mackay.

BOTTOM: 'Not the Nine O'Clock News' arrived on the scene October 1979 with (l to r) Mel Smith, Rowan Atkinson, Pamela Stephenson and Griff Rhys Jones. The award-winning comedy series took an off-beat look at news and current events.

THIS PAGE

TOP: February 1985 marked the start of the BBC's top-rated soap opera, 'EastEnders'. The residents of Albert Square are seen here in their local, The Queen Vic.

BOTTOM: 'Bluebell', which started its run in January 1986, was a dramatised version of the life of Miss Bluebell and her Parisian night club dancers. It starred Carolyn Pickles as Miss Bluebell and Philip Sayer as her husband, Marcel.

OPPOSITE PAGE

TOP: The 'Live Aid' charity concerts, broadcast partly simultaneously from Wembley Stadium and from the John F. Kennedy Stadium in Philadelphia in July 1985 were seen live throughout the world. Some countries received the transmission through one of the American networks and others, covering about 500 million people, through the BBC.

BOTTOM LEFT: The political thriller 'Edge of Darkness' starred Bob Peck as policeman, Ronald Craven who became involved in high-level secret double dealing in the nuclear industry. It won two awards at the annual British Academy of Film and Television Arts (Bafta) ceremony in March 1986: best drama serial and best actor award for Bob Peck.

CENTRE RIGHT: 'Only Fools and Horses' won the 1986 Bafta award as the best comedy series. It stars (l to r) Nicholas Lyndhurst as Rodney, David Jason as Del Boy and in a 1983 episode, Lennard Pearce as Grandad.

BOTTOM RIGHT: 'Gardeners' World', one of a number of gardening series, started in January 1968. In a June 1984 edition, presenter, Geoff Hamilton, began giving tips on starting a garden from scratch.

Sir Alec Guinness starred as spy-catcher, George Smiley, in John le Carre's 'Smiley's People' which began in September 1982.

TOP INSET: The lunchtime magazine programme 'Pebble Mill at One' from Birmingham ran from 1972 until May 1986. The presenters in a March 1978 edition were (l to r) David Seymour, Jan Leeming, Marian Foster and Donny Macleod.

BOTTOM INSET: The relationship between the recently widowed Audrey Fforbes-Hamilton (Penelope Keith) and the nouveau-riche Richard de Vere (Peter Bowles) was the theme for the comedy 'To the Manor Born'. The series began in June 1979.

THIS PAGE

A surprise meeting between actress, Coral Browne and the former spy, Guy Burgess, in Moscow in 1958 was the theme for the award winning film, 'An Englishman Abroad' televised in November 1983. Alan Bates played Burgess and Coral Browne who had been touring in 'Hamlet' when she met the real Burgess, played herself.

THIS PAGE

TOP: Victoria Wood (l) and Julie Walters starred in 'Victoria Wood: As Seen on TV' in a wide range of comedy roles. Victoria Wood herself and the series won top awards in the 1986 Bafta ceremony.

CENTRE: A drama documentary 'The Fools on the Hill', based on events leading up to the opening of television in November 1936, was transmitted during the anniversary celebrations. In this scene were Anthony Calf as Leslie Mitchell and Maev Alexander as Jasmine Bligh wearing make-up for Baird studio transmissions (see pp 21, 22).

BOTTOM: A highlight of the television anniversary year was the wedding of Prince Andrew and Miss Sarah Ferguson at Westminster Abbey in July. As with the wedding of the Prince and Princess of Wales the outside broadcast enjoyed a worldwide audience.

OPPOSITE PAGE

A dramatisation of Anita Brookner's Booker prize-winning novel 'Hotel du Lac' was televised in March 1986. The play, a character study of people in a small hotel at the end of the season starred (l to r) Julia McKenzie as Jenifer Pusey and Googie Withers as her mother.

TOP: Tales of 'Postman Pat' on his rounds in the small town of Greendale joined the children's television schedules in September 1981.

CENTRE: The snooker programme, 'Pot Black' enjoyed a 17 year run starting in July 1969. In this line up for the start of the 16th series in January 1984 were (l to r)(back) Jimmy White, Willie Thorne, Tony Knowles, John Spencer, Steve Davies, Silvino Francisco, Mark Wildman, Kirk Stevens, Terry Griffiths, Vic Batham (referee), Ted Lowe (commentator), John Williams (referee). (Front) Alan Weeks (commentator) Eddie Charlton, Ray Reardon, David Taylor, Dennis Taylor, Tony Meo.

BOTTOM: In February 1985, Terry Wogan (r) began his three-times weekly chat show 'Wogan'. One of his guests in a January 1986 edition was the political commentator, Sir Robin Day.

INDEX